# DECADES OF THE 20TH CENTURY

# 1970s

ELDORADO INK

# DECADES OF THE 20TH CENTURY

1900s

1910s

1920s

1930s

1940s

1950s

1960s

1970s

1980s

1990s

# DECADES OF THE
# 20TH CENTURY

# 1970s

ELDORADO INK

Published by Eldorado Ink
2099 Lost Oak Trail
Prescott, AZ 86303
www.eldoradoink.com

Milan Bobek, Editor
Judith C. Callomon, Historical consultant
Samuel J. Patti, Consulting editor

Printed and bound in Slovenia

**Publisher Cataloging Data**
1970s / [Milan Bobek, editor].
        p. cm. -- (Decades of the 20th century)
        Includes index.
        Summary: This volume, arranged chronologically, presents key events that have shaped the decade, from significant political occurrences to details of daily life.
        ISBN 1-932904-07-7
        1. Nineteen seventies   2. History, Modern--20th century--Chronology   3. History, Modern--20th century--Pictorial works
I. Bobek, Milan   II. Title: Nineteen seventies   III. Series
        909.82/7--dc22

Picture research and photography by Anne Hobart Lang and Rolf Lang of AHL Archives. Additional research by Heritage Picture Collection, London.

# CONTENTS

# REVOLUTION AND LIBERATION

Against a background of civil war, coups, and oppression, technology moves forward: Commercial flight goes supersonic, computers invade everyday life, and "test-tube" babies are born. Mars is found to be apparently barren; humanity loses interest in space and turns its attention to the pollution of the environment and the impact of technology on the ecological balance. Feminism becomes at once more militant and mainstream. The first signs of religious fundamentalism emerge in the Middle East.

RIGHT: Demonstrators rally to protest against the war in Vietnam.

## 1970–1979

### KEY EVENTS OF THE DECADE

- IDI AMIN SEIZES POWER IN UGANDA
- GREENPEACE BEGINS ITS PROTESTS
- TROUBLE IN NORTHERN IRELAND
- END OF VIETNAM WAR
- WATERGATE SCANDAL
- BLACK SEPTEMBER OLYMPICS
- PINOCHET COUP IN CHILE
- THE COD WAR
- POL POT REGIME IN CAMBODIA
- CIVIL WAR IN THE LEBANON

- THE STEVEN BIKO INCIDENT
- ELVIS PRESLEY DIES
- FIRST TEST-TUBE BABY BORN
- CIVIL WAR IN NICARAGUA
- HOMOSEXUAL RIGHTS
- ISLAMIC REVOLUTION IN IRAN
- THREE MILE ISLAND
- RUSSIA INVADES AFGHANISTAN

WORLD POPULATION 3,693 MILLION

# DÉTENTE IN THE EAST AND DEATH ON THE CAMPUS

The new decade sees continued protest over the American involvement in Vietnam, despite promises of withdrawal. Anti-war demonstrations continue and in the United States four students are shot dead by the National Guard on the campus of Kent State University in Ohio. West Germany's chancellor, Willy Brandt, initiates détente with East Germany. The Palestinian Black September movement is formed and attacks Jordan. *Apollo 13* proves as unlucky as its number and the astronauts in it get back to Earth on a wing and a prayer. Political heavyweights Charles de Gaulle and Gamal Nasser of Egypt leave the world stage.

## 1970

| | | |
|---|---|---|
| **Mar** | **19** | First meeting of East and West German heads of state |
| **Apr** | **10** | Paul McCartney announces that he is leaving the Beatles |
| | **17** | U.S. *Apollo 13* Moon mission is aborted after an explosion. The crew returns safely in the lunar module |
| **Sept** | **5** | In Chile, Marxist Salvador Allende is elected president |
| | **14–27** | War in Jordan between Jordanian Army and Palestinian militia |
| | **18** | Jimi Hendrix, American guitar great, dies of drug related causes at the age of 27 |
| **Sept** | **28** | In Egypt, President Nasser dies at age 52 of a heart attack |
| **Oct** | **4** | Janis Joplin dies of a drug overdose at the age of 27 |
| | **5** | Anwar Sadat is elected President of Egypt |
| **Nov** | **9** | Former French president Charles de Gaulle dies at age 79 |
| | **17** | Soviet space probe *Luna 17* lands on the Moon and deploys an unmanned exploration vehicle |
| **Dec** | **7** | West Germany and Poland sign treaty recognizing Poland's frontier |

ABOVE: The staff at Houston Mission Control celebrate the safe return of the *Apollo 13* crew.

## GERMAN DETENTE
The first meeting between Willy Brandt of West Germany and Willi Stoph of East Germany, at Erfurt in East Germany, starts the process of détente in Europe.

## DEATH ON THE CAMPUS
U.S. National Guards shoot dead four anti-war demonstrators on Kent State University campus in Ohio. Anti-war protests continue throughout the United States against U.S. involvement in the Vietnam War.

## ALLENDE WINS
Salvador Allende wins the presidential election in Chile and becomes the first democratically elected Marxist head of state in the world. He begins a program of reform, including the nationalization of copper mines owned by U.S. subsidiaries.

## BLACK SEPTEMBER
After militant Palestinians hijack three aircraft to Jordan, the Jordanian government evicts the Palestinians and regains control of the kingdom in a month of struggle which will be known as Black September.

## TROUBLED INDEPENDENCE FOR ADEN
After four years, British troops withdraw from Aden as independence approaches. The withdrawal sees conflict with the National Liberation Front (NLF). The British suffer 57 dead and 651 wounded. Local civilian casualties include 280 dead and 922 wounded.

## POWER CHANGE IN EGYPT
Egyptian president Gamal Abdel Nasser (b. 1918) dies and is succeeded by Anwar Sadat.

RIGHT: Aquanauts replicate conditions in space, spending 20 days in *Tektite 11*, an underwater habitat designed and funded by NASA.

## HIPPIES IN HOLLAND
Hippies are cleared from the Dutch National Monument in Dam Square, Amsterdam. The permissive Dutch city has become the alternative capital of Europe for the young, called *asfaltjeugd*, or "asphalt youth," because they sleep in the city's parks and squares.

## POLISH BORDER ASSURED
West Germany and Poland sign a treaty recognizing the current border between Poland and Germany, thus reassuring Poland about any possible German moves to reacquire land lost after the war.

## SPACE DRAMA
U.S. spacecraft *Apollo 13*, on its way to the Moon, is crippled by an explosion. The astronauts on board, James Lovell, John Swigert, and Fred Haise, guided by ground control in Houston and watched by the world, manage to swing the damaged craft around the Moon and return safely to Earth, using the lunar module Aquarius as a "lifeboat."

## I KNOW WHY THE CAGED BIRD SINGS

American writer Maya Angelou's autobiography is released and includes her account of sexual and racial oppression (raped at the age of eight, followed by a period of muteness). It marks her emergence as a major writer. Further volumes of her autobiography will follow.

## LUNOKHOD EXPLORES THE MOON

Russian unmanned spacecraft *Luna 17* lands an eight-wheeled vehicle, *Lunokhod 1*, on the Moon. It travels more than ⅔ mile exploring the surface by remote control.

## M*A*S*H

Robert Altman makes moving comedy out of events in the Korean War. Two surgeons in a mobile army hospital try to keep themselves sane with joking, womanizing, and subverting authority. Although set in Korea, the parallels with Vietnam are inescapable. The film forms the basis of a popular TV series.

## ESCALATION IN IRELAND

In Belfast, the Provisional Irish Republican Army kills a British soldier on October 31. This signals war between the illegal army and the British government.

## VENUS PROBE

The Russian space probe *Venera 7* drops a package of instruments on to the surface of the planet Venus; it sends back information for 23 minutes before the fierce heat destroys it.

## THE FEMALE EUNUCH

Australian writer, academic, and feminist Germaine Greer argues that characteristics in women traditionally valued by men (delicacy, passivity, etc.) show "castration" of the true female personality, something in which women have colluded. The book becomes a key feminist text.

ABOVE: The film version of *One Day in the Life of Ivan Denisovich*, Solzhenitsyn's grim description of life in a Soviet prison gulag.

RIGHT: Burt Bacharach wins an Oscar for his music score for the 1969 movie *Butch Cassidy and the Sundance Kid*.

## ENVIRONMENTAL AWARENESS

The first Earth Day is celebrated by 20 million Americans, who attend teach-ins and rallies, and participate in schemes to clean up the environment.

## CROW

This collection confirms Ted Hughes' early promise as the major English poet of his generation. The sinister figure of Crow, mythically memorable, surviving through hostility to humankind, is one of the most powerful creations in the literature of the time.

## ACCIDENTAL DEATH OF AN ANARCHIST

In this play, Italian Marxist Dario Fo draws influence from traditional European forms (farce, *commedia dell'arte*) to bring a satirical sharpness to the theater.

## FLOPPY DISKS

U.S. computer company IBM introduces floppy disks for storing computer information.

## CROWDED SKIES

China and Japan launch their first space satellites.

## COMPUTERIZED CATALOGUE

The Smithsonian Institution in Washington, D.C. begins to compile a computerized catalogue of all U.S. plants.

## EXPLORING EARTH'S CRUST

Russian scientists begin drilling a deep well on the Kola Peninsula, north of the Arctic Circle, to examine the Earth's crust. They plan to drill down 9 miles.

### CHARLES ANDRE JOSEPH MARIE DE GAULLE (1890–1970)

Former French president and founder in exile of the Free French Army (1940), Charles de Gaulle, has died. The World War I army officer who headed postwar provisional governments and became president of the Fifth Republic in 1958 is credited with resolving the Algerian crisis and restoring stability to postwar France. His handling of the situation in May 1968 seemed at first to guarantee his continued popularity, but he resigned last year after a disastrous referendum vote of no-confidence.

# ECOWARRIORS AND BLACK HOLES

The Canadian pressure group for the environment, Greenpeace, carries out its first act of confrontation in Alaska. In Switzerland, women get the vote at last. East Pakistan declares itself independent and chooses a new name, Bangladesh, while in Uganda, Idi Amin seizes power. U.S. astronauts visit the Moon again and the U.S.S.R. puts a space station into orbit. Homosexuals assert their rights and the term Gay Pride is coined. In space, black holes, the imprints of collapsed, gravity-sucking stars, are discovered.

## 1 9 7 1

| | | |
|---|---|---|
| **Jan** | 10 | French fashion queen Coco Chanel dies at age 87 |
| | 25 | Idi Amin seizes power in Uganda |
| **Feb** | 7 | Swiss women get the right to vote |
| | 15 | U.K. introduces a decimal currency |
| **Apr** | 6 | Russo-American composer Igor Stravinsky dies aged 88 |
| | 19 | Soviets put *Salyut 1*, the first space station, into orbit |
| | 25 | In the U.S., 200,000 people demonstrate against the Vietnam War in Washington, D.C. |
| | 25 | Awami League declares East Pakistan independent as Bangladesh |
| **Jun** | 28 | The Supreme Court reverses the conviction of Muhammad Ali for refusing induction into the Army |

| | | |
|---|---|---|
| **Jul** | 1 | West Indies cricketer and statesman Learie Constantine (Baron Constantine) dies aged 69 |
| | 6 | Jazz great Louis "Satchmo" Armstrong dies at the age of 71 |
| **Aug** | 9 | Internment without trial introduced in Northern Ireland |
| **Sep** | 11 | Nikita Khrushchev dies in obscurity at the age of 78 |
| | 30 | Canadian ecowarriors Greenpeace stage their first protest in Alaska |
| **Nov** | 12 | President Nixon ends the U.S. offensive role in Vietnam |
| | 15 | The People's Republic of China is formally admitted to the U.N. |
| **Dec** | 17 | End of the Indo-Pakistan War |

ABOVE: Feminist writer Betty Friedan leads NOW, the National Organization of Women.

### GAY LIBERATION GROWS
Gay liberation groups emerge in major cities in North America, Australia, and Western Europe, following the foundation of active American groups who led a successful campaign to challenge injustices perpetrated against homosexuals. Gay Pride marches raise public consciousness of the predicament of gay and lesbian people.

### MADMEN AND SPECIALISTS
Nigerian writer Wole Soyinka's volume of verse and prose shows his versatility as a writer. His diverse writings stress the need for a distinctively African written culture, crossfertilized by, but independent from, that of Europe.

### UNDERNEATH THE ARCHES
London-based artists Gilbert and George impersonate English music hall artists Bud Flanagan and Chesney Allen (one of whose best-known routines was a song and dance duet called "Underneath the Arches") to create the first "living sculpture." The work causes hilarity and controversy, which is presumably what the artists intend.

### DIGITAL WATCH
U.S. engineers George Theiss and Willy Crabtree develop the first digital watch, powered by a vibrating quartz crystal.

### UAE FORMED
The United Arab Emirates is formed by six sheikhdoms as Britain leaves the Persian Gulf after 150 years. Bahrain and Qatar become independent in their own right.

ABOVE: Gloria Steinem, former Playboy Bunny, campaigns for women's rights.

ABOVE: Women demonstrate to legalize abortion and for the right to choose what to do with their own bodies.

LEFT: Women demonstrate in support of the Equal Rights Amendment to the U.S. Constitution.

ABOVE: Flags of 126 nations flutter outside the United Nations building in New York City. China joins this year.

### BANGLADESH GAINS INDEPENDENCE

Led by Sheikh Mujibur Rahman, the Awami League wins all the seats in East Pakistan in the general election in December 1970 and begins talks on a new constitution for the province. As talks break down, Rahman declares independence as Bangladesh, in protest against neglect of the province by West Pakistan, establishes a government in exile in Calcutta in April. Tension rises during the year, until border clashes between India and East Pakistan lead to a brief war in December. Indian forces defeat the Pakistani Army. As a result, Pakistan is divided and Bangladesh gains its independence.

### THE HARDER HOUSE

Eccentric American architect Bruce Goff designs this house for a Minnesota turkey farmer. The building combines natural and "postmodern" materials (stone, wood, and shingle on the one hand, orange roof covering and mirror mosaic on the other) to create a unique synthesis.

RIGHT: The *Apollo 14* launch vehicle on the pad. Alan B. Shepard, Stuart A. Roose and Edgar D. Mitchell are the astronauts on this mission.

### BLACK HOLES FOUND

Astronomers discover black holes in space. These have been predicted by English physicist Stephen Hawking. Black holes are collapsed stars whose gravity is so strong that not even light can escape from them, so they cannot be observed visually.

### "POCKET" CALCULATORS

U.S. company Texas Instruments introduces the first pocket calculator, the Pocketronic. It goes into mass production at once, weighing $2^1/_2$ pounds and costing $150.

### ORBITING MARS

In November, U.S. space probe *Mariner 9* goes into orbit around Mars, the first planet to be explored in this manner. *Mariner 9* sends back 7,329 photographs and allows scientists to make accurate maps of the planet.

### GABRIELLE (COCO) CHANEL
### (1883–1971)

French couturier Coco Chanel has died. She founded her couture house in Paris in 1924 and created the classic chemise dress and the Chanel suit with its collarless jacket. She was also responsible for the "little black dress" that remains chic cocktail party wear and her own perfumes, especially Chanel No. 5. After a long period of retirement, she took up her career again during the 1950s.

LEFT: Beat poet Alan Ginsberg meets his admirers.

## FIRST SPACE STATION
On April 19 the Russians put *Salyut 1*, the first space station, into orbit. The idea is to establish a kind of base camp in space so that teams of cosmonauts can work in shifts.

## COSMONAUT DEATHS
Three Russian cosmonauts are found dead in their spacecraft *Salyut II* after an apparently normal landing; Loss of air from the cabin is blamed for their deaths.

BELOW: Dr. Daniel Ellsberg, the whistle-blower of Watergate.

ABOVE: The distinctive Smiley Face logo is the icon of the LSD-taking classes. It is destined for a revival in the clubs of the 1980s.

## INTERNMENT IN IRELAND

The British government introduces internment without trial in an attempt to prevent terrorism. It leads to riots and hunger strikes.

ABOVE: British rock star Rod Stewart performs in the United States.

## HOME VIDEO

Philips launches the first video cassette recorder (VCR) for home use. The ½ inch tape plays for 1 hour.

## MOON ROCKS BROUGHT BACK

U.S. spacecraft *Apollo 14* and *Apollo 15* bring back Moon rocks for analysis. Members of the *Apollo 15* crew, David Scott and James Irwin, gather theirs during a drive in a lunar roving vehicle or "Moon buggy."

## CHINA IN THE U.N.

China takes its seat at the U.N. in place of Taiwan, which has held the seat since 1945.

---

### IGOR FYODOROVICH STRAVINSKY (1882–1971)

Composer, pianist, and conductor Igor Stravinsky has died in New York. Born in Russia, he left for France after the revolution and later became an American citizen, having moved to the United States in 1939. He first came to fame with his ballets for Diaghilev's Ballets Russes: *The Firebird* (1910), *Petrushka* (1911), and *The Rite of Spring* (1913). Other works include *Pulcinella* (1919–1920) and *The Rake's Progress* (1951), and many orchestral, voice, and chamber compositions. He incorporated such diverse influences as Russian folk music, American jazz, Verdi, Monteverdi, Baroque music, and music of the Viennese school. His burial will be in Venice, close to Diaghilev.

# BLOODY SUNDAY AND BLACK SEPTEMBER

Sunday January 30 in Londonderry, Northern Ireland, sees 13 civilians killed, leading to decades of murders and bombings. President Nixon goes to China to make an alliance with the world's third superpower. In Washington, D.C., burglars break into the Watergate Hotel to plant bugs. At the Munich Olympics, Palestinian activists murder 11 Israeli athletes. In Burundi, rival tribes, the Hutus and the Tutsis, slaughter each other. FBI chief J. Edgar Hoover dies and some very surprising secrets emerge from his closet.

## 1972

| | | |
|---|---|---|
| **Jan** | 30 | "Bloody Sunday" in Londonderry, Northern Ireland: British troops fire on demonstrators, killing 13 |
| | 30 | Pakistan leaves the Commonwealth |
| **Feb** | 2 | Winter Olympics open in Tokyo, Japan |
| | 21 | U.S. president Nixon begins visit to China |
| **Mar** | 2 | U.S. launches *Pioneer 10* to photograph Jupiter |
| | 24 | Britain suspends Northern Ireland parliament and imposes direct rule |
| **May** | 28 | The Duke of Windsor (ex-King Edward VIII) dies at age 77 |
| **Jun** | 17 | Intruders try to bug Democratic Party headquarters in the Watergate Hotel in Washington, D.C. |
| **Jul** | 23 | U.S. launches *Landsat 1*, which orbits Earth taking many photographs |
| **Aug** | 2 | Belgian statesman Paul Spaak dies at age 72 |
| | 4 | President Idi Amin of Uganda orders all Asian citizens to leave |
| | 26 | The 20th Olympic Games open in Munich, Germany |
| **Sep** | 3 | Bobby Fischer defeats Russian Boris Spassky to claim the World Chess Championship |
| | 4 | American swimmer Mark Spitz wins his seventh gold medal in Munich |
| | 8 | Arab terrorists murder 11 members of the Israeli Olympic team |
| **Dec** | 2 | Labour Party wins Australian general election |
| | 7 | Last Apollo mission to the Moon |

ABOVE: Commander John W. Young salutes the Stars and Stripes planted on the Moon during the *Apollo 16* mission.

BELOW: *Apollo 16*'s lunar module, known as *Orion*.

RIGHT: President Nixon goes to China and meets Chou En-Lai, premier of the People's Republic.

## WATERGATE

Burglars are arrested breaking into the Democratic Party headquarters in the Watergate Hotel. Over the next year, it is established that they were working for the committee to reelect the president, Richard Nixon, in 1972. Nixon wins easily against anti-war campaigner and Democratic candidate George McGovern.

## BLOODY SUNDAY

In Londonderry, Northern Ireland, British paratroopers open fire on unarmed demonstrators protesting against the British policy of interning Irish Republican Army (IRA) members and kill 13 civilians. Bloody Sunday marks the low point of relations between the Catholic community and the British Army and leads to a huge increase in violence across the province. In March, as a direct result of the violence, the Northern Irish parliament is suspended and direct rule is imposed from London.

## NIXON IN CHINA

In a historic move, U.S. president Richard Nixon visits China and meets the Communist leadership. The visit leads to a thaw in relations between the two superpowers, both of which have reason to work together against the Soviet Union.

ABOVE: Olga Korbut wins three Olympic golds in Munich.

ABOVE: Writer Stokely Carmichael, a prominent activist in the black civil rights movement.

### UGANDANS EXPELLED
President Idi Amin expels 50,000 Asians with British passports from Uganda, claiming that they are sabotaging the national economy. The Asians all leave within three months, causing economic ruin in Uganda as factories close and vital services stop.

### AUSTRALIA TURNS TO THE PACIFIC
Gough Whitlam leads the Labour Party to victory in the general election in Australia. He radically changes Australian foreign policy away from the United States and toward Asia by recognizing China, giving Papua New Guinea its independence, pardoning Vietnam draft dodgers, and ending national service.

### GAY MINISTRY
A ministry to the gay community, founded in 1968 in Los Angeles by Troy Perry, an expelled Pentecostal preacher, is expanding across America. The Evangelical Lutheran Church of the Netherlands declares that there is no obstacle to the appointment of gay ministers.

---

### JOHN EDGAR HOOVER
### (1895–1972)

The American J. (John) Edgar Hoover, for 48 years director of the Federal Bureau of Investigations, has died. In this role he was responsible for establishing the national fingerprint file and the FBI crime laboratory. He clamped down both on the gangster rackets of the 1920s and 1930s and the postwar spread of Socialist and Communist sympathizers. He had been exempted from civil service retirement regulations to allow him to retain his post. Later it will be revealed that he had been a homosexual while publicly demonstrating homophobic tendencies.

### LASERVISION
The Dutch firm of Philips introduces a system of recording on plastic discs using lasers. The system is later marketed as LaserVision.

### WINTER OLYMPICS IN JAPAN
Disputes over amateur status lead to the disqualification of a skier and the withdrawal of the Canadian ice hockey team from the 11th Winter Games in Sapporo, Japan. Revenue from TV rights climbs to $8.47 million, three times the 1968 sum.

### SPEED OF LIGHT REMEASURED
U.S. scientist Kenneth M. Evenson produces a more accurate measurement of the speed of light than has been possible hitherto: 186,282.3959 miles per second.

### BLACK SEPTEMBER OLYMPICS
Palestinian terrorists hijack the 20th Olympiad in Munich, Germany. Their attack on the Israeli team in the Olympic Village leaves 11 athletes and a policeman dead. German authorities botch a rescue attempt as the terrorists and hostages transfer from helicopters to a plane at a military airfield. Five of the eight Palestinians are killed. The International Olympic Committee refuses to bow to violence and, with the backing of the Israeli government, the games continue with flags at half-mast. In competition, U.S. swimmer Mark Spitz claims an astounding seven golds. Soviet gymnast Olga Korbut is the crowd favorite and wins three golds.

### IT'S A WRAP
Bulgarian-born French artist Christo wraps a section of the coastline of Australia. The enormous artwork uses some 1 million square feet of plastic sheeting and attracts publicity all over the world.

### ENDGAME
Maverick Bobby Fischer is crowned the first American chess world champion after defeating Russian Boris Spassky in Iceland.

ABOVE: Commander Gene Cernan test drives the Moon buggy on the *Apollo 17* mission.

### EQUIVALENT 8
U.S. sculptor Carl André's *Equivalent 8* is a sculpture consisting of a pile of 120 bricks. It is bought by London's Tate Gallery, to derisive comments from press and public alike. The sculptor explains his work in terms of making "cuts in space."

### LANDSAT 1 LAUNCHED
The United States launches *Landsat 1*, otherwise called the Earth Resources Test Satellite, which photographs the Earth's surface in a series of strips and covers all the globe, except the two Poles, every 18 days. The photographs will yield vital information about crop growth, deforestation, floods, and other data.

### CAT SCANNER
British engineer Godfrey Hounsfield and South African physicist Allan Cormack invent the Computerized Axial Tomography scanner (known as CAT). It uses computer technology to produce images of the brain and becomes an important diagnostic tool.

### THE U.N. AND THE ENVIRONMENT
A United Nations Conference on the Human Environment meets in Stockholm to discuss environmental issues.

### IN A FREE STATE
Trinidadian-born British writer V.S. Naipaul's novel explores identity through three linked narratives of people outside their native territory. Its bleak vision is typical of the author's later work.

### OFF TO JUPITER
NASA launches *Pioneer 10*, a spaceprobe designed to take close-up photographs of the planet Jupiter. It is scheduled to fly past the giant planet in December 1973.

### MASSACRES IN BURUNDI
Rebel Hutus massacre thousands of their compatriots from the minority Tutsi tribe who are in government. The Tutsis retaliate and much slaughter ensues.

# POLLUTION AND WASTE

ABOVE: Pesticides and agribusiness dominate farming.

BELOW: Wrecked automobiles pile up, a symbol of Western waste.

ABOVE: Dallas, Texas, where the automobiles and the road seem to cover the planet.

ABOVE: Atmospheric pollution from a steelworks.

ABOVE: Raw sewage discharging into a river.

# PEACE IN VIETNAM AND WAR IN THE MIDDLE EAST

Peace treaties are signed to end the wars in Vietnam and its neighbor Laos. The United States will take many years to recover from the war it did not win. In Chile, General Pinochet stages a coup and President Allende is murdered. Egypt and Syria attack Israel in the Yom Kippur War. In the North Atlantic, Icelandic fishing trawlers battle with the British fleet over disputed territories. CITES is established to monitor the trade in endangered species and the European Community admits Denmark, the United Kingdom, and Ireland.

## 1973

| | | | | | |
|---|---|---|---|---|---|
| **Jan** | 1 | Denmark, Ireland, and the United Kingdom join the European Community | **Sep** | 21 | Junta headed by General Augusto Pinochet seizes power in Chile and President Allende is assassinated |
| | 22 | Former U.S. president Lyndon B. Johnson dies at age 64 | **Oct** | 6 | Arab countries attack Israel on Yom Kippur, the Jewish Day of Atonement |
| | 22 | George Foreman knocks out Joe Frazier in the second round to win the heavyweight championship | | 10 | U.S. Vice President Spiro T. Agnew resigns after tax evasion scandal |
| | 27 | Cease-fire in Vietnam is signed in Paris by North and South Vietnam, the Viet Cong guerrillas, and U.S. | | 21 | The Oakland A's defeat the New York Mets to win the World Series |
| | | | | 24 | Yom Kippur War ends |
| **Apr** | 6 | United States launches *Pioneer 11* to take close-ups of Jupiter and Saturn | **Nov** | 3 | United States launches *Mariner 10* to photograph Venus and Mercury |
| | 8 | Spanish painter Pablo Picasso dies at age 91 | **Dec** | 1 | David Ben-Gurion, former Israeli prime minister, dies at age 87 |
| **May** | 25 | United States launches *Skylab*, its first space station | | 6 | Gerald Ford is sworn in as the new Vice President |

## PEACE IN VIETNAM

A cease-fire is declared in Vietnam as a peace agreement is signed in Paris between the United States and North and South Vietnam. The U.S. agrees to withdraw all its troops and exchange prisoners of war.

## COUP IN CHILE

President Allende of Chile is ousted and killed in a coup by General Pinochet. The new military government introduces martial law and imprisons its opponents, driving thousands into exile.

## YOM KIPPUR WAR

Egypt and Syria attack Israel during the religious Yom Kippur holiday. Israel fights back, crossing the Suez Canal and threatening to cut off the invading Egyptian Army. A cease-fire is arranged by the UN, but oil-rich Arab nations raise the price of oil by 70 percent in protest against U.S. support for Israel. As a result, fuel shortages and inflation hit all the Western economies.

## THE SECOND BATTLE OF WOUNDED KNEE

Members of the American Indian Movement seize Wounded Knee on the Sioux Reservation in South Dakota to protest against Indian treaties broken by the U.S. government. Fighting to end the occupation results in two deaths, with many injuries and arrests.

## CEASE-FIRE IN LAOS

In this former French colony, the Pathet Lao, backed by the North Vietnamese, fight the Royalist Laotian government. Since the Ho Chi Minh trail passes through Laos, the U.S. backs the Royalist forces against the 35,000 strong Pathet Lao. A cease-fire is agreed in 1973 when South Vietnam falls to the North. In 1975 Laos will come under complete Pathet Lao control.

## INNER PLANETS

U.S. space probe *Mariner 10* is launched, designed to observe Venus and Mercury, the two planets that orbit between Earth and the Sun.

ABOVE: Former president Lyndon Baines Johnson dies this year.

## EC EXPANDS

The United Kingdom, Ireland, and Denmark join the European Community (EC) after the new French government of Georges Pompidou relaxes its veto on British entry. Nine nations are now members of the EC.

## OPEN STUDY

The first graduates of the Open University, founded in the U.K. in 1969 for mature students without formal qualifications to gain university-level education, receive their degrees.

## CITES ESTABLISHED

A Convention on International Trade in Endangered Species (CITES) is drawn up at a conference to end the trade, held in Washington, D.C., and is signed by representatives of 80 countries.

## RIDING ROUGH TERRAIN

A mountain bike is designed for riding the slopes of canyons in California by the Marin County Canyon cycling club.

---

### PABLO CASALS
### (1876–1973)

Spanish-born cellist Pablo Casals has died in Puerto Rico, where he has lived since 1956. He gave his first performances in Barcelona cafes. Ever since his first American tour in 1901, he has been recognized as the world's leading cellist, playing as a soloist and with the pianist Alfred Cortot and violinist Jacques Thibaut. In exile from Franco's Spain, he founded the Prades Festival in France before settling in Puerto Rico.

---

ABOVE: Richard M. Nixon is sworn in for his second term in presidential office. It will only last for two years.

ABOVE: John Mitchell and his attorney at the Watergate trial.

ABOVE: Nixon's chief of staff, Robert Haldeman, testifies at the Watergate trial.

### SYDNEY OPERA HOUSE

Jørn Utzon's opera house is finally completed. Its construction has been a saga of bumbles and U-turns; the authorities accepted Utzon's sketches before anyone had worked out how to build the roofs. They have to swap the roles of the two main auditoriums and have to start a lottery to pay for it. But they get as great a civic symbol as any in the world.

### A LITTLE NIGHT MUSIC

One of the most successful of U.S. composer Stephen Sondheim's early musicals, *Night Music*, has a tragicomic plot based on Bergman's film *Smiles on a Summer Night*. The score is notable for its operatic vocal requirements and for being almost entirely in waltz time. The lyrics demonstrate Sondheim's perennial wit.

### DAY FOR NIGHT

French director François Truffaut's film is about filmmaking. The loving depiction of both the pleasures and frustrations of the art explores all aspects from technical details and props to the relationship between actor and director, and the distinction between movie and reality.

### GRAVITY'S RAINBOW

American writer Thomas Pynchon produces his largest book, set at the end of World War II. Its fantastic take on reality reminds some critics of Latin American magic realism.

### MUSIC FOR PIECES OF WOOD

Steve Reich's work is a typical minimalist piece, scored for five tuned claves, which play separate repeated patterns of notes. This is one of the most extreme forms of minimalism.

### THE COD WAR

Hostilities break out between Iceland and the U.K. when Icelandic territorial waters are expanded from 50 miles to 200 miles, so encroaching on fishing grounds used by the British. British fishing boats are escorted into the zone by a super-tug and the situation rapidly escalates, involving the Royal Navy and Icelandic gunboats. There are riots outside the British embassy in Reyjkjavik.

### ICELANDIC VOLCANO

A volcano erupts on the island of Heimaey and all 5,000 inhabitants have to leave their homes in the middle of the night.

### SKYLAB

America's first space station, *Skylab*, is launched and goes into orbit 270 miles above the Earth. Three different crews are sent in turn to *Skylab* during the year. It delivers information about Earth's resources and the structure of the Sun.

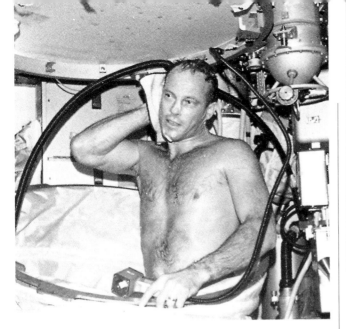

ABOVE: Almost normal life is possible for the crew inside the space station *Skylab 3*.

RIGHT: Astronaut Jack Lousma works outside *Skylab 3*. He is one of a three-man team.

## JUPITER AND SATURN TO BE EXPLORED

NASA launches *Pioneer 11*, a space probe designed to take close-up pictures of both Jupiter (in 1974) and Saturn (in 1979).

## GENETIC ENGINEERING

U.S. chemists Stanley H. Cohen and Herbert W. Boyer use the process of genetic engineering to make bacteria produce small quantities of insulin. This represents the beginning of genetic engineering.

## DOLPHIN TRIUMPH

The Miami Dolphins cap a perfect 17 victory season by beating the Washington Redskins in Super Bowl VII. The Dolphins are the only team in NFL history to go undefeated.

ABOVE: Redford and Newman in the Oscar-winning film *The Sting*.

## DEATHS IN THE ARTS

Edward G. Robinson (b. 1893), the screen gangster, U.S. writer and Nobel Prize winner Pearl S. Buck (b. 1892), French painter Jacques Lipchitz (b. 1891), U.S. Kung Fu star Bruce Lee (b. 1940), English playwright Noel Coward (b. 1899), film director John Ford (b. 1895), author J.R.R. Tolkien (b. 1892), and poet W.H. Auden (b. 1907) all die this year.

## POLITICAL DEATHS

Former U.S. President Lyndon Baines Johnson (b. 1908), Jeanette Rankin, the first woman in Congress (b. 1880), and Fulgencio Batista, the Cuban dictator (b. 1901) all die this year.

## SMALL IS BEAUTIFUL

American economist E.F. Schumacher introduces the idea of alternative technology in his bestseller *Small is Beautiful: a Study of Economics as if People Mattered*.

## TELETEXT DEMONSTRATED

British TV companies demonstrate teletext news and information pages in addition to normal programs.

### PABLO PICASSO
### (1881–1973)

Pablo Picasso, the prolific painter, sculptor, and ceramic artist, who was born in Spain in 1881 but who has for many years lived and worked in France, has died. Together with Georges Braque, he developed cubism and has had a hugely powerful influence on the direction of modern art. He began designing costumes and sets for the Ballets Russes from 1917 and became a Communist during World War ll. His work *Guernica*, painted in 1937 during the Spanish Civil War, has become a byword for anti-war art.

# RESIGNATION BEFORE IMPEACHMENT

The fallout from the Watergate scandal forces President Nixon to resign before he is impeached. A military coup in the dictatorship of Portugal leads to democracy and independence for Portuguese colonies Goa, Mozambique, and Portuguese Guinea. In Cyprus, President Makarios is overthrown and Turkey invades. Civilian rule reasserts itself in Greece. In Ethiopia, Haile Selassie is deposed and exiled and the remains of humankind's oldest-known ancestor are found. The propellant in aerosol cans, CFC, is unmasked as the agent that is blowing a hole in the ozone layer. From space, *Mariner 10* sends back images of Mercury and Venus.

## 1974

| | | | | | |
|---|---|---|---|---|---|
| **Feb** | **8** | Three U.S. astronauts return after a record 84 days aboard *Skylab 3* | **July** | **24** | Constantine Karamanlis returns from exile to form civilian government in Greece |
| **Apr** | **4** | Henry Aaron hits home run number 715 to break Babe Ruth's record | **Aug** | **9** | Because of the Watergate scandal, Richard M. Nixon becomes the first U.S. president to resign; Vice President Gerald Ford succeeds him |
| **July** | **1** | Argentine president Juan Perón dies at 78; succeeded by his wife Isabel | | | |
| | **15** | In Cyprus, the National Guard overthrows President Makarios; former terrorist Nicos Sampson takes over | **Sep** | **12** | A military coup overthrows Emperor Haile Selassie of Ethiopia |
| | **20** | Turkey invades Cyprus | **Nov** | **12** | "Lucy," ancient ancestor of human beings, is found in Ethiopia |
| | **23** | Greek military government resigns | | | |

## MOZAMBIQUE INDEPENDENT

Since 1962, the Front for the Liberation of Mozambique (FRELIMO) has been fighting the 40,000-strong Portuguese Colonial Army. In 350 actions, the Portuguese inflict 4,000 casualties on FRELIMO. However, under the Marxist Samora Machel, the 10,000 men of FRELIMO are able to profit from the 1974 military coup in Portugal and seize larger areas of Mozambique. Machel negotiates from strength with the Portuguese and is elected the first president of Mozambique in 1975. Instability will dog the early years of the new country as Rhodesian-backed members of the anti-Communist MNR (Mozambican National Resistance) sabotage oil supplies and communications and South African forces raid southern Mozambique by attacking African National Congress (ANC) bases.

ABOVE: President Nixon puts a brave face on the Watergate affair as he addresses a meeting of Young Republicans. Future president George H.W. Bush is shown in the background.

## NIXON RESIGNS

President Nixon resigns rather than face impeachment for his role in the Watergate burglary. He is succeeded by Vice President Gerald Ford, who promptly pardons Nixon for his misdemeanors. Several Nixon aides go to jail after their trial.

## PERON DIES

On the death of President Juan Perón, his wife Isabel becomes president, the first woman to hold such a job anywhere in Latin America. She proves to be a weak leader and is toppled by a military coup in March 1976.

ABOVE: Joint U.S. and Soviet space vehicles on exhibition.

## COUP IN PORTUGAL

A military coup led by General de Spinola overthrows the Portuguese government in the "Revolution of Flowers" and begins moves towards democracy. The Socialist leader, Mario Soares, returns from exile and leads his party to victory in the first democratic elections in April 1975. An attempted Communist coup by left-wing soldiers is defeated in November 1975, ensuring the survival of Portuguese democracy.

## PARTITION IN CYPRUS

The National Guard overthrows President Makarios and installs former EOKA terrorist Nicos Sampson, who is in favor of union with Greece. Turkey promptly invades the north of the island and partitions it, setting up a separate state in February 1975.

## SPACE MISSION RECORD

On February 8, three U.S. astronauts return to Earth after having spent 84 days in *Skylab 3*, a space record. This is the last mission to the space station.

## GERMAN TRIUMPH

The Dutch, playing free-flowing "total soccer," are everyone's choice to win the World Cup in West Germany, but the hosts take the title. Germany beats Holland 2–1 in the final.

## GUINEA-BISSAU INDEPENDENT

Nationalists, the African Party for the Independence of Guinea and Cape Verde (PAIGC), have been fighting for independence from the colonial power Portugal since 1963. By 1973, PAIGC had gained control of two-thirds of Portuguese Guinea and the military coup in Lisbon in 1974 gives the country independence.

## INCLUDE ME OUT

Sam Goldwyn, legendary film mogul, dies. Born Samuel Goldfish in Poland in 1882, he began life as a glove salesman. His films were always aimed at the family and he was famous for his "Goldwynisms" (such as, "A verbal contract is not worth the paper it's written on."), not all of which he actually said.

## HAILE SELASSIE DEPOSED

Emperor Haile Selassie is deposed in a left-wing military coup after a massive famine in 1973 weakens his rule. The new government introduces massive reforms, executes its enemies, and kills Selassie in August 1975.

## TOUR DE FORCE

Belgian cyclist Eddie Merckx crosses the line first in the Tour de France cycling race for the fifth time in six years. In the seven tours Merckx enters he wins 35 stages and wears the leader's yellow jersey for 96 days, both of which are records.

## EARLY FOOTPRINTS

At Laetoli, near Olduvai Gorge in Tanzania, fossils of hominids who lived three million years ago are found. The earliest known hominid footprints and the oldest human artifacts have been discovered by British archeologist Richard Leakey and his team.

## RUMBLING WITH THE GREATEST

Muhammad Ali regains the heavyweight boxing title in a fight against George Foreman in Kinshasa, Zaire. "The Rumble in the Jungle" goes eight rounds before Foreman is counted out.

## ANOTHER MOON FOR JUPITER

U.S. astronomer Charles T. Kowall discovers another satellite of Jupiter, which is subsequently named Leda.

ABOVE: The tree-sized petition carrying signatures of people who believe that President Nixon should be impeached.

## MARINER VISITS PLANETS
U.S. space probe *Mariner 10* passes Venus and then proceeds to pass Mercury on March 29. It then orbits the Sun and passes Mercury two more times on September 21 and March 16, 1975.

## EASY SHAVES
Disposable lightweight plastic razors are developed by Gillette in Boston.

## ANCIENT AMERICAN
Anthropologists using new dating techniques discover that a human skull found in Southern California is 48,000 years old. It shows that people have lived in North America far longer than previously thought.

## THE DUKE BOWS OUT
U.S. jazz pianist Duke (Edward Kennedy) Ellington dies. One of the great men of big band jazz, his career lasted for 55 years.

## AEROSOLS ACCUSED
U.S. scientists Sherwood Rowland and Mario Molina point out that the chlorofluorocarbons (CFCs) used as propellants in aerosol cans could damage the ozone layer high above the Earth.

## ANOTHER QUARK
U.S. physicist Burton Richter discovers another quark (a subunit of protons and neutrons); this one is given the name of charmed quark.

RIGHT: The fearsome teeth of a shark loom out of the screen to terrify moviegoers in the blockbuster film *Jaws*.

## GREEK CIVIL RULE RETURNS
As a result of the debacle in Cyprus, the Greek military government resigns and civilian rule is restored in mainland Greece. The ex-premier, Constantine Karamanlis, returns from exile in Paris to form a new government, winning elections in November. In December, Greece votes to become a republic, ending any chance of a restoration of the monarchy.

## "LUCY" DISCOVERED
U.S. anthropologist Donald C. Johanson discovers in Ethiopia the fossil skeleton of a female *Australopithecus afarensis*, an ape-like ancestor of human beings. She is nicknamed "Lucy" after the Beatles song, "Lucy in the Sky with Diamonds."

## POMPIDOU DIES
The president of France, Georges Pompidou, dies of an unnamed illness.

## STANDING TALL IN CANADA
Toronto's stunning telecommunications tower, the CN tower, becomes the world's tallest freestanding structure. It is 1,815 feet high.

## SOLZHENITSYN EXPELLED
The first part of *The Gulag Archipelago* is published and its author, Alexander Solzhenitsyn, is expelled from the Soviet Union. This marks the height of Solzhenitsyn's fame as a Soviet dissident and prophet.

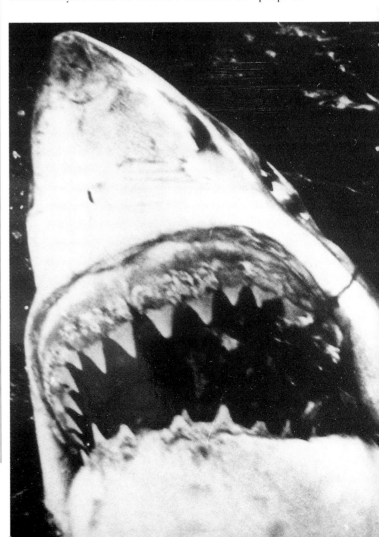

# THE WATERGATE SCANDAL

ABOVE: Domestic Council Chief John D. Ehrlichmann confers with his lawyer during the trial for his part in the Watergate affair.

ABOVE: John Ehrlichmann faces the press. Nixon's aides share the blame for the greatest political scandal of the 1970s.

LEFT: John Dean testifies at the trial of men implicated in the Watergate affair.

ABOVE: Senator Sam Erwin leads questioning in what has become known as the Watergate trial.

ABOVE: Mountains of files and tapes containing damaging evidence are on their way to the Watergate trial.

LEFT: President Nixon is left to face the music alone as even his lawyer testifies against him.

# HANDSHAKE IN SPACE

The Vietnam War finally comes to an end. The Khmer Rouge, under Pol Pot, seizes Cambodia and embarks on a bloodbath. Indonesia invades East Timor. The United States and Soviet Union link up in space when two of their spacecraft dock in Earth's orbit. The United States sends out space probes in search of life on Mars while Soviet space probes send back the first-ever pictures from the planet Venus. General Franco dies and archaeologists find a 2,000 year old "army."

## 1975

| | | |
|---|---|---|
| Feb | 21 | John Mitchell, H.R. Haldeman, and John Ehrlichman, three former top aides to President Nixon, are sentenced to prison |
| April | 5 | President of Nationalist China, Chiang Kai-shek, dies at age 88 |
| | 17 | Khmer Rouge takes control of Cambodia |
| | 30 | Vietnam War ends; Saigon surrenders to North Vietnam; mass evacuation of Americans |
| June | 6 | Israelis attack Lebanon |
| | 12 | Indian prime minister Indira Gandhi found guilty of corruption |
| | 25 | Mozambique gains independence |
| July | 11 | Archaeologists discover ancient terra cotta "army" in China |
| | 19 | U.S. astronauts and Soviet cosmonauts meet in space |

| | | |
|---|---|---|
| Aug | 1 | Helsinki Conference on security and cooperation in Europe |
| Sep | 18 | Patty Hearst is apprehended in San Francisco and will be charged with bank robbery |
| | 22 | Sara Jane Moore fires a gunshot at President Ford in an assassination attempt |
| Oct | 1 | Muhammad Ali defeats Joe Frazier in the "Thrilla in Manilla." |
| Nov | 10 | Angola becomes independent of Portugal |
| | 20 | General Franco dies in Spain at age 73 |
| | 22 | Monarchy is restored to Spain |
| | 24 | Civil war begins in Angola |
| Dec | 7 | Indonesian troops invade East Timor |

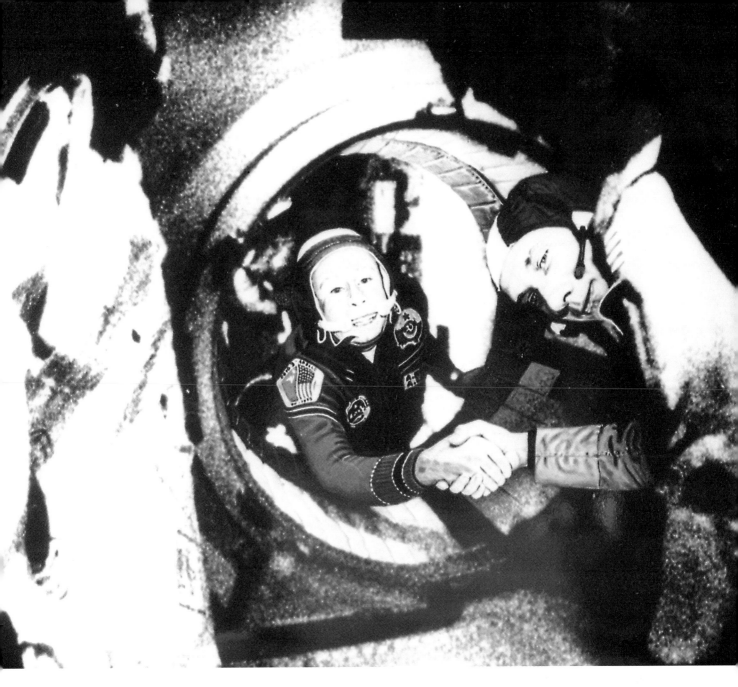

## KHMER ROUGE SEIZE POWER

In Cambodia, Communist Khmer Rouge forces led by Pol Pot (1926–1998) seize power in Cambodia and begin a four year reign of terror. Within months, thousands of Cambodians are executed. The cities are emptied out and people forced to work on the land as the new government attempts to rebuild Cambodian society from Year Zero. More than 3.5 million people, half of the total population, die during famine, fighting, and political killings.

## INDONESIA INVADES EAST TIMOR

Indonesian paratroopers invade the former Portuguese colony of East Timor, just before it gains independence. The country is engaged in a civil war between the Timorese Democratic Union (UDT), backed by the Timorese Democratic People's Union (APODETI), and the Communist-backed Revolutionary Front for Independence (FREITLIN). The Indonesian move halts the fighting but is a land grab on the part of Indonesia. It provokes protests from the East Timorese and leads to violent repression and human rights abuses.

ABOVE: Russian and American astronauts meet in space in the joint U.S. and Soviet mission to dock in Earth's orbit.

## VIETNAM WAR ENDS

Communist North Vietnam finally takes over South Vietnam, ending the 15 year Vietnam War. The old southern capital of Saigon is renamed Ho Chi Minh City in honor of the Communist leader.

## COLONIES INDEPENDENT

Mozambique gains its independence from Portugal, followed by the Cape Verde Islands, Angola, and São Tomé and Príncipe. In South America, the former Dutch colony of Surinam gains its independence from the Netherlands.

## MISSIONS TO MARS AND VENUS

The United States launches two space probes, *Viking 1* and *Viking 2*, to look for signs of life on Mars. In October, Russian space probes *Venera 9* and *Venera 10* send back the first pictures of the surface of Venus.

ABOVE: The U.S.S.R.'s *Soyuz* spacecraft and launch vehicle on their way to the launch pad.

ABOVE RIGHT: An artist's idea of what the *Soyuz* spacecraft will look like as it orbits the Earth.

## CIVIL WAR IN ANGOLA

Within two weeks of gaining independence, civil war intensifies in Angola. Thousands die as rival groups struggle for control of the country. The Soviet Union and Cuba back the Marxist Popular Movement for the Liberation of Angola (MPLA). The United States supports two non-Marxist groups, the National Angolan Liberation Front (FNLA) and National Union for the Total Independence of Angola (UNITA).

## INDIRA GANDHI FOUND GUILTY

Prime Minister Indira Gandhi (1917–1984) is found guilty of electoral corruption. She declares a state of emergency, imposing censorship and imprisoning opposition leaders. The state of emergency lasts until January 1977, when she calls for an election. She loses badly to the opposition Janata Party, but she regains power in 1980.

## TERRA-COTTA ARMY

In China, archaeologists make a remarkable discovery when they uncover a vast army of 6,000 terra cotta soldiers, near the ancient Chinese capital of Xian. The soldiers date back some 2,000 years and were probably made to guard the tomb of the first emperor in 206 B.C. The terra-cotta soldiers stand in rows. Each one is different from the other and was probably modeled on a real person.

## NATIONS JOIN FOR HUMAN RIGHTS

In Helsinki, Finland, more than 30 European nations, plus the United States and Canada, join together to sign the Final Act of the Conference on Security and Cooperation. They promise to avoid the use of force in disputes and to respect human rights.

## DEMOCRATIC SPAIN

General Franco dies and Spain becomes a monarchy once more as he is succeeded by King Juan Carlos. The new king begins moves to introduce democracy, granting an amnesty to all opponents of the previous government.

## LEBANON CIVIL WAR

Seeking a pretext to attack the Palestine Liberation Organization (PLO) in southern Lebanon, the Israeli government launches operation "Peace for Galilee" in June. The attack takes them up to Beirut and costs the Israelis 368 killed and 2,388 wounded. Some 17,800 PLO, Syrians, and civilians are killed and more than 30,000 wounded. By 1976, the PLO has evacuated Lebanon and abandoned heavy weapons.

## MID-ATLANTIC DIVES

Three research submersibles make a total of 43 dives on the Mid-Atlantic Ridge, taking photographs and collecting rock samples.

## BLACK TENNIS SUCCESS

At Wimbledon, Arthur Ashe (1943–1993) beats fellow American Jimmy Connors to become the first male black Wimbledon champion.

## DISTANT GALAXIES

The enormity of space is emphasized when U.S. astronomer Hyron Spinrad discovers that a faint galaxy he is studying is approximately eight billion light years away from us. In Holland, Dutch astronomers at Leiden University map radio galaxy 3C236, the largest object in the universe, spanning eighteen million light years.

## HANDSHAKE IN SPACE

U.S. astronauts in an Apollo spacecraft link up with Soviet cosmonauts in a Soyuz spacecraft some 140 miles above the Atlantic Ocean. One from each crew, U.S. captain Tom Stafford and Soviet Alexei Leonov, shake hands through the hatches of their respective spacecraft. While linked together, the crews carry out joint scientific experiments and visit each other's crafts.

## HEALTHY EATING

A healthy vegetarian diet becomes popular in the United States and Britain. It is influenced by the macrobiotic diet, based on brown rice, natural salt, and green tea, which was fashionable in the 1960s. Its importance is also reinforced by a report from a British doctor indicating a link between bowel cancer and a low-fiber diet.

## THE BOOK OF SAND

This collection of stories by Argentinian writer Jorge Luis Borges (1899–1986) confirms his international stature as a master of serious puzzles, play with truth and identity, and the role of time in fiction. His fiction is newly fashionable for its similarity to magic realism.

## NEW SHOPPING CENTER

SITE Projects Inc. have designed a stunning new shopping center, the Almeda-Genoa in Houston, which exemplifies their witty style. The facade seems to be crumbling, with holes, piles of bricks, and jagged edges, a witty impersonation of a modern ruin.

## RITUEL, IN MEMORIAM BRUNO MADERNA

French modernist composer Pierre Boulez (b. 1925) has created a work in memory of his Italian colleague, Bruno Maderna. The performing ensemble is divided into eight groups, dominated by a group of brass instruments, which play alternate sections. The work impresses with its manipulation of chords and rhythms.

### FRANCISCO FRANCO
### (1892–1975)

General Franco, leader of the Nationalists during the Spanish Civil War, and dictator of Spain since 1939, has died in Madrid. In 1969, he announced that the monarchy would be restored on his death.

ABOVE: Arthur Ashe is the first black male player to win the singles title at Wimbledon.

## GAY COMMERCIALS

In the Netherlands, gays advertise openly as a result of a gay recognition campaign conducted by COC (an organization for men) and MVM (Man-Vrouw Maatschappij or Man-Woman Society) for lesbians.

## STREAKING

A new craze, streaking, has hit both sides of the Atlantic. In both the U.S. and Britain, sports events are being interrupted by the arrival of naked people, both men and women, "streaking" across the playing areas.

## PCs ON SALE

In the United States, the Altair, the world's first personal computer (PC), is launched.

ABOVE: A scene from *The Godfather II*, winner of six Oscars.

# APARTHEID VIOLENCE AND SUPERSONIC FLIGHT

Chairman Mao, Chinese cult figure and leader of the revolution, dies. Police fire on students in Soweto, South Africa, and African nations boycott the Olympic Games. Israeli commandos carry out a lightning rescue of hostages in Uganda. Concorde, the uniquely designed supersonic jet, begins regular passenger flights. Drug laws are liberalized in Holland.

## 1976

| | | |
|---|---|---|
| **Jan** | **21** | Concordes fly from Paris to Rio de Janeiro, and London to Bahrain, launching the start of regular Concorde passenger flights |
| **Feb** | **4** | Winter Olympics open at Innsbruck, Austria |
| | **27** | Polisario Front declares independence of Western Sahara |
| **Mar** | **24** | Military coup in Argentina overthrows President Perón |
| **April** | **14** | Western Sahara partitioned between Morocco and Mauritania |
| **June** | **16** | South African police gun down black students in Soweto. |
| **July** | **3** | Israeli commandos rescue hostages at Entebbe airport, Uganda |
| **July** | **20** | U.S. *Viking* space probe lands on Mars |
| **Aug** | **8** | Women launch a peace movement in Northern Ireland |
| **Sept** | **9** | Chairman Mao Zedong dies in China at age 83 |
| **Oct** | **23** | "Gang of Four," including Mao's widow are arrested in China |
| **Nov** | **2** | Democrat Jimmy Carter wins the U.S. presidential election |
| | **15** | Parti Québécois wins large victory in Quebec elections, Canada |
| | **27** | Northern Irish women lead 30,000-strong peace march through London |
| **Dec** | **20** | Mayor Richard Daley of Chicago dies of a heart attack at age 74 |

ABOVE: Operation Sail brings the tall ships from 28 nations to New York City. This is the Portuguese ship *Sagres*.

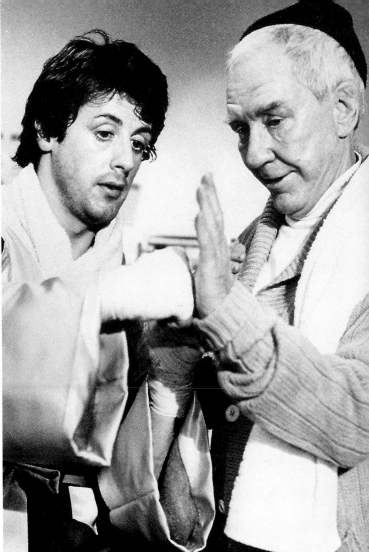

ABOVE: Surprise film hit of the year is *Rocky*, written by and starring Sylvester Stallone. It will be followed by a dynasty of *Rockys*.

## WESTERN SAHARA DISPUTE

Following Franco's death, the Spanish colony of Western Sahara is divided between Morocco and Mauritania. However, a nationalist pro-independence movement known as Polisario, formed in 1973, rejects the partition and wages a guerrilla war. Mauritania later withdraws, leaving Morocco in sole control of the colony and fighting a lengthy campaign against Polisario, who fight for its independence.

## KILLINGS IN SOWETO

Protest breaks out in the black township of Soweto, South Africa. This follows a government decision that secondary school subjects must be taught in the Afrikaans language, which black South Africans see as the language of oppression. Police open fire and seventy six students are killed and more than 1,000 are injured. Subsequently, the government drops its controversial education plans.

## DUTCH LIBERALIZE DRUG LAWS

The drug laws are liberalized in the Netherlands with the revision of the Opium Act of 1928. Possession of soft drugs now has the lowest penalties in a new table of penalties for drug offenses.

## ENTEBBE RESCUE

Israeli commandos rescue 110 people held hostage in Entebbe airport, Uganda, after their Air France plane is hijacked by Palestinian guerrillas and flown to Entebbe. All seven hostage-takers and 20 Ugandan soldiers are killed in the raid, with the loss of only three hostages. Most of the Ugandan Air Force is destroyed on the ground by the Israelis.

## SUPERSONIC BIRD

Air travel reaches supersonic speeds when two Anglo-French supersonic Concorde turbo jets, one taking off from Paris, one from London, begin a regular passenger service across the Atlantic. With its distinctive drooping nose and looking like a fantastic bird, Concorde cruises at 1,461 miles per hour and can cross the Atlantic in three hours.

## QUEBEC VOTES

In Canada, the Parti Québécois, which is seeking an independent Quebec, wins a large majority in the state elections. Led by René Levesque, it promises a referendum on independence from Canada. In May 1980, Quebec votes by a large majority to remain in Canada.

ABOVE: American John Naber wins gold in the 100m men's backstroke event at the Montreal Olympics.

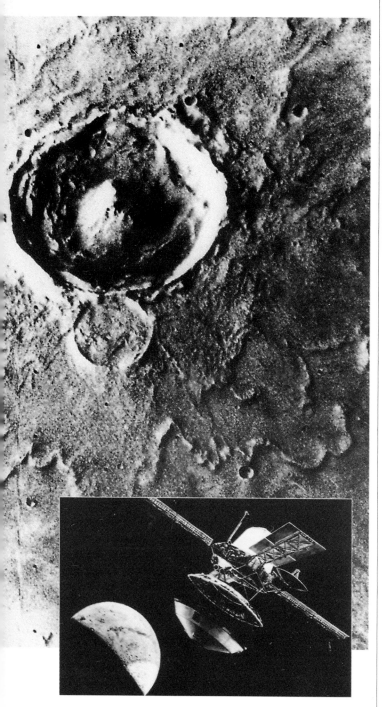

ABOVE: The surface of Mars is photographed by *Viking 1*. The inset shows a model of the Viking spacecraft in orbit round the red planet.

### ARGENTINA "DIRTY WAR"
In Argentina, a military coup overthrows President Isabel Perón and a three person junta led by Lt. Gen. Jorge Videla is installed. The constitution is amended and the junta takes action against left-wing activists or those suspected of left-wing sympathies. Political and trade union activity is banned. Between 1976 and 1983, an estimated 10,000 to 15,000 people are murdered or "disappeared" during internal repression.

### EINSTEIN ON THE BEACH
American composer Philip Glass (b. 1937) has produced a new opera, *Einstein on the Beach*. In typically minimalist mode, very little happens, although the opera has hypnotic qualities. It cements Glass's position as a major opera composer.

### NO LIFE ON MARS
The U.S. space probe *Viking I* lands on Mars and sends close-up pictures of the surface of Mars back to Earth. These reveal a barren surface littered with rocks and no signs of life. But there are signs of dry river beds, showing that water once existed there. The space probes also scoop up soil samples and analyze them for the presence of microorganisms.

### ROOTS
American author Alex Haley (1921–92) has published a new book, *Roots*. It is the saga of a black African sold into slavery in the U.S. and of his descendants. In this novel, Haley, who has already published a biography of black American activist Malcolm X, depicts poverty and racial hatred as modern forms of enslavement for black people. It becomes the basis for the first TV mini-series.

### WINTER OLYMPICS
The Winter Olympics are held at Innsbruck in Austria, using the facilities from 1968, after Denver withdraws. Austrian hero Franz Klammer takes gold in the men's downhill event while Rosi Mittermaier wins the women's downhill and a further gold and silver for Germany.

## WOMEN PRIESTS

The Episcopal Church, the American wing of the Anglican church, approves the ordination of women Christian priests. Previously, in July 1974, four American Episcopalian bishops ordained 11 women priests in contravention of Church law.

## IRISH WOMEN MARCH FOR PEACE

The women of Belfast, in Northern Ireland, launch a peace campaign. Subsequently, they organize a protest march against continued fighting in Northern Ireland, which is joined by 30,000 people. American folk singer Joan Baez (b. 1941) gives support.

## SYMPHONY OF SORROWFUL SONGS

Polish composer Henryk Górecki produces a new symphony, *Symphony No 3* or *Symphony of Sorrowful Songs*. Its use of traditional form (canons) and a tonal idiom mark a turning-away from the harshly modernist style of the composer's earlier works.

## GYMNAST SHINES AT BOYCOTTED GAMES

Amid strict security and unfinished building, the Olympic Games open in Montreal, Canada. African nations boycott the games in protest at New Zealand's rugby connection with South Africa. Romanian gymnast Nadia Comaneci, who is only aged 14, gives a dazzling display, winning five medals and the affection of the spectators.

## HITE REPORT

U.S. feminist Shere Hite (b. 1943) publishes *The Hite Report: A Nationwide Study of Female Sexuality*. The result of five years of research, it includes information from 3,000 women on all aspects of female sexuality. It challenges many traditional assumptions about women's sexuality and causes a sensation.

---

## MAO ZEDONG (MAO TSE-TUNG) (1893–1976)

Chinese Marxist leader Mao Zedong has died. Mao was one of the founders of the Chinese Communist party when it was formed in 1921. He was a leader in the long struggle against the Japanese and then the Kuomintang Nationalists. In 1949, he became first chairman of the new People's Republic of China. In 1958, he launched the disastrous Great Leap Forward of agricultural reforms and resigned as head of state later that year. But he remained party chairman, and in 1962, his *Little Red Book*, containing his many sayings and thoughts, was fervently studied all over China. In 1966, now a cult figure, he set alight the Cultural Revolution with the aim of overthrowing the enemies of Socialism. At the end of this period, 1970, he became supreme commander of the nation.

---

ABOVE: Computer games make their debut with this exciting game of virtual tennis. Over 200 such games are available.

## LEGIONNAIRES DISEASE

The first outbreak of a new type of pneumonia occurs at an American Legion convention in Philadelphia; it is named Legionnaires Disease.

## MOUNTAIN BIKE RACE

The first official mountain bike race takes place on a 2 mile course on Mount Tamalpais, California.

## MOON ROCK DATED

Researchers discover that Moon rock sample 76535 is at least 4.54 billion years old.

ABOVE: The Washington Redskins battle with the New York Jets.

ABOVE: Rock fans chill out among the laid-back crowd.

ABOVE: Some fans find inspiration for their own musical efforts.

# STADIUM ROCK CONCERTS

ABOVE: Rock legends Lynyrd Skynyrd electrify the audience at an open-air concert.

# STAR WARS AND MICROSOFT

Black South African activist Steven Biko is killed while in police custody. African nations boycott the Olympic Games. Charter 77 calls for human rights in Czechoslovakia. Nineteen year old Bill Gates founds Microsoft. The inside-out Pompidou Center is a dramatic new Paris landmark. A new film, *Star Wars*, opens to rapturous audiences. A medical development, balloon angioplasty, offers new treatment for heart disease. Elvis Presley, "the King of Rock and Roll," dies.

## 1977

| | | | | | |
|---|---|---|---|---|---|
| **Jan** | 7 | Charter 77 calls for human rights in Czechoslovakia | **Aug** | 16 | King of Rock, Elvis Presley, dies in Memphis at the age of 42 |
| | 17 | Gary Gilmore is executed in the United States, the first execution for ten years | | 19 | Comedian Groucho Marx dies at the age of 77 |
| | | | | 30 | David Berkowitz, the "Son of Sam" killer, is arrested and charged with the murder of 6 people in New York |
| **Feb** | 18 | Archbishop of Uganda murdered by Idi Amin's forces | | | |
| | | | **Sep** | 7 | United States and Panama sign a treaty returning Canal Zone to Panama |
| **Mar** | 10 | Astronomers discover rings of planet Uranus | | | |
| | 21 | Indira Gandhi, after ruling India for 11 years, is voted from office in a landslide defeat | | 12 | Black South African activist Steven Biko is killed while in police custody |
| | 27 | Jumbo jets collide in the Canary Islands, killing more than 570 people | **Oct** | 14 | Singer Bing Crosby dies of a heart attack in Spain at the age of 73 |
| **June** | 15 | First democratic elections in Spain since 1936 lead to victory for center parties | **Nov** | 21 | Egyptian President Sadat visits Israel on a peace mission |

ABOVE: American tennis star Jimmy Connors smashes his way to victory in the men's singles at Wimbledon.

## BIKO KILLED

Black consciousness leader Steven Biko is killed in custody by South African police. He was one of a number of black leaders who have been arrested under new security legislation. A postmortem reveals brain injuries. Some 15,000 people attend his funeral. Biko's death causes an international outcry, increasing international pressure on the apartheid National Party government, which wins a record majority in white-only elections in November.

## EGYPT TALKS PEACE WITH ISRAEL

President Sadat (1918–1981) of Egypt offers peace to Israel, alienating other Arab states. At the end of November, he visits Israel and addresses the Knesset, the Israeli parliament.

## AIR DISASTER

Two jumbo jets collide at Tenerife airport, in the Canary Islands. More than 570 people are killed, most of them American vacationers. It is the worst disaster in the history of aviation.

## CHARTER 77 CALLS FOR HUMAN RIGHTS

In Czechoslovakia, 240 intellectuals and dissidents sign Charter 77, calling for the Czech government to implement the human rights it agreed to support as part of the 1975 Helsinki Declaration. Several of the signatories are arrested and the leader, Jan Potocka, dies after police interrogation.

## POMPIDOU CENTER

Italian Renzo Piano and Englishman Richard Rogers design a revolutionary new-style arts center in Paris, the Pompidou Center. It provokes considerable controversy. All the services (drains, wiring, elevators, heating ducts) are suspended on the outside of the building, making a striking decorative amalgam. This leaves the interior free for broad uninterrupted exhibition spaces.

## STAR WARS

A new science fiction film is released and is a smash success. Directed by U.S. filmmaker George Lucas (b. 1944), it is called *Star Wars*. It features the latest in special effects as well as starring a princess, a dashing hero, and two robots, R2D2 and C-3PO. Two more films will follow, with more in the pipeline.

## CANAL BACK TO PANAMA

U.S. president Jimmy Carter and General Omar Torrijos of Panama sign a treaty to return the Canal Zone to Panamanian control by 2000.

### SIR CHARLES SPENCER (CHARLIE) CHAPLIN (1889–1977)

English comedian and filmmaker Charlie Chaplin has died. After a tough childhood he became a member of the Fred Karno vaudeville company and went with them to Hollywood, where he was to make a film every two weeks between 1914 and 1916. He created the flat-footed, baggy-trousered, bowler-hatted tramp still regarded with affection today. His comic talent was at its best in the silent cinema and he will be remembered for classics such as *The Kid* (1920), *The Gold Rush* (1925), and *City Lights* (1931).

TOP AND LEFT: The Trans-Alaska oil pipeline under construction. It will be 800 miles long.

ABOVE: An earthmoving machine helps to build the 360 mile service road for the Alaska pipeline.

## ARCHBISHOP MURDERED

In Uganda, President Idi Amin's regime becomes increasingly repressive when Amin's forces murder the human rights advocate, the Most Reverend Janani Luwum, archbishop of Uganda.

## BALLOON ANGIOPLASTY

Swiss doctor Andreas Grünzig devises balloon angioplasty. This involves inserting a tiny inflatable balloon into a blocked artery to clear it.

### WERNHER VON BRAUN
### (1912–1977)

German-born rocket expert Wernher von Braun has died. Having perfected the V-2 rockets used by Germany during World War ll, he and his team surrendered at the end of the war and took up residence in the United States, where he continued his work. An American citizen since 1955, he was responsible for the development of the satellite *Explorer l* (1958). As director of the Marshal Space Flight Center (1960–1970), he developed the rocket used in the 1969 *Apollo S* Moon landing.

## MARIA MENEGHINI CALLAS (1923–1977)

The great operatic soprano Maria Callas has died in Paris. Born in New York City into a Greek family, she studied at the Athens National Conservatory from the age of about 15. Her debut was in Athens in 1940. She sang many roles from Brunnhilde to Violetta and her prima donna status was secured by her first performance at La Scala in 1950 in *Aida*. She worked with conductors such as Giulini and Von Karajan, and with producers such as Visconti and Zeffirelli, drawing record breaking audiences. Her last performance was in *Tosca* at Covent Garden in 1965, but she continued to make records and give occasional concerts. Her unsurpassed musicianship was accompanied by great dramatic talent. Her glamour made her the focus of attention in private as well as public life.

BELOW: Greek-born opera diva Maria Callas, one of the most celebrated singers of our time, dies this year in her Paris home of a heart attack at the age of 53.

### MICROSOFT FOUNDED

Paul Allen (b. 1953) and Bill Gates (b. 1955) set up a new computer software company, Microsoft. Gates is only 19. He will be a millionaire within ten years and Microsoft will be the world's largest producer of micro-computer software.

### LIFE IN THE OCEAN DEEP

U.S. scientists aboard the submersible *Alvin* discover worms, crabs, and fish living in warm water from vents in the Galapagos Rift near Ecuador, far from sunlight and feeding on bacteria.

### DEATH PENALTY BACK

The death penalty returns to the United States when convicted murderer Gary Gilmore is executed by firing squad. This is the first execution to take place for ten years and follows considerable protest and public debate.

### APPLE RIPENS

The Apple II, the first personal computer sold ready assembled, goes on the market.

### DEMOCRATIC SPAIN

The first democratic elections since 1936 are held in Spain. They lead to victory for Adolfo Suárez (b. 1932) and the Democratic Center party.

ABOVE: Elvis Presley in the Vegas years that preceded his early death, apparently from an overdose of prescription drugs.

RIGHT: Rock music becomes a big industry, with vinyl records leading the way.

### ELVIS AARON PRESLEY
### (1935–1977)

Elvis Presley, the world's most popular pop star, has died suddenly at his home in Memphis of the accumulated effects of overweight and narcotics. Presley was born in Mississippi and first sang in his local Pentecostal church choir. He came to fame with his first single "That's All Right Mama" in 1954 and will always be remembered for his 1956–58 rock and roll classics such as "Heartbreak Hotel," "Hound Dog," and "Don't be Cruel," and the songs from the 1958 films of the same names, "Jailhouse Rock" and "King Creole." In the 1960s, the King of Rock and Roll took to crooning and gave up live performances. In the 1970s, he once again was performing frequently to huge audiences in Las Vegas nightclubs.

### URANUS RINGS FOUND

United States astronomers discover a ring system around the planet Uranus. In 1985, *Voyager 2* will confirm these findings and show that these rings are standard features for the gas planets of our solar systems

### GOSSAMER CONDOR FLIES

In California, cyclist Bryan Allen pedals an 81 pound aircraft, the *Gossamer Condor*, around a 1.19 mile figure eight course in 6 minutes and 22.5 seconds to win an $87,000 prize for the fastest human-powered flight.

### SMALLPOX ERADICATED

The world's last case of the disease smallpox occurs in Somalia, following a campaign by the World Health Organization to eradicate it. Formal eradication is announced in 1980.

# TEST-TUBE BABIES BORN

The world's first "test-tube" baby is born, following the development of *in-vitro* fertilization. Astronomers observe a new moon, that of the planet Pluto, and U.S. space probes begin mapping the surface of Venus. Civil war breaks out in Nicaragua. Egypt and Israel make peace at Camp David. The world's worst oil spill to date occurs and environmentalists become increasingly concerned about the impact of CFCs on the ozone layer.

# 1978

| | | |
|---|---|---|
| **Mar** | 1 | Communist support enables a new Italian government in "Historic Compromise" |
| | 8 | U.N. recognizes March 8 as International Women's Day |
| | 16 | World's worst oil spill occurs off the coast of France |
| **May** | 20 | United States launches space probe *Pioneer Venus I*, which goes into orbit around Venus |
| **June** | 13 | Proposition 13 is passed by California voters and cuts property taxes |
| | 22 | Pluto's moon, Charon, is discovered |
| **July** | 25 | World's first "test-tube" baby born |
| **Aug** | 17 | First manned transatlantic crossing in a hot-air balloon |
| | 22 | Kenyan statesman Jomo Kenyatta dies aged about 89 |
| **Aug** | 22 | Sandinistas seize control of the parliament building in Nicaragua |
| **Sep** | 5 | Peace summit at Camp David between U.S. president Carter, President Sadat of Egypt, and Israeli prime minister Begin |
| | 17 | U.S. boxer Muhammad Ali beats Leon Spinks |
| | 29 | Pope John Paul I, who had just been elected to the papacy on August 26, dies of a heart attack at age 65 |
| **Oct** | 16 | Archbishop of Cracow, Karol Wojtyla, becomes the first non-Italian Pope in more than 400 years |
| **Nov** | 29 | More than 900 people die in a cult mass suicide in Guyana |
| **Dec** | 25 | Vietnam begins full-scale invasion of Cambodia |

ABOVE: Women march in Washington to protest against the government's seven year delay in ratifying the Equal Rights Amendment.

## HISTORIC COMPROMISE

A "Historic Compromise" is made between Christian Democrats and Communists in Italy, allowing Prime Minister Andreotti (b. 1919) to take power with Communist Party support. The Italian Communist Party is the biggest in Western Europe and the deal gives it influence in government for the first time since the war.

## CAMP DAVID PEACE SUMMIT

A summit held at the U.S. presidential retreat at Camp David achieves peace between Egypt and Israel. In the deal between President Anwar Sadat of Egypt and the Israeli prime minister, Menachem Begin, Israel agrees to give back the Sinai Peninsula to Egypt. The arrangement is heavily criticized in the Arab world.

## POLISH POPE

Polish born John Paul II (b. 1920) becomes the first non-Italian pope in 435 years after the deaths of both Paul VI and John Paul I. A conservative, John Paul II uses his office to attack Communist control of Eastern Europe and liberal tendencies inside the Church.

## MAJOR OIL SPILL

The Amoco *Cadiz* supertanker runs aground in storms in the Atlantic off the Brittany coast and splits in two. Some 80,000 tons of crude oil devastate French beaches, wildlife habitats, and fishing grounds. It is the worst oil spill to date.

## NICARAGUAN CIVIL WAR

In August, guerrillas of the Sandinista National Liberation Front fight the government of President Anastasio Somoza in Nicaragua, taking over the parliament building in Managua. By September, the rebellion is suppressed at a cost of 5,000 killed and 10,000 wounded.

## TEST-TUBE BABIES

Louise Brown, the world's first "test-tube" baby, is born in the U.K. This follows work by physiologist Robert Edwards and gynecologist Patrick Steptoe, who have devised a method of fertilizing an egg outside the human body. The new technique is known as *in-vitro* and involves fertilizing an ovum in a test-tube. The embryo is then replaced in the mother's uterus where it develops naturally. Some months later, in October, a second "test-tube" baby is born in Calcutta, India, to Bela and Pravat Agarwal.

## PLUTO'S MOON OBSERVED

U.S. astronomers James W. Christy and Robert S. Harrington of the U.S. Naval Observatory, Washington, D.C., discover that the planet Pluto has a moon. It is named Charon. Earlier attempts to detect a moon have been unsuccessful because Pluto is so remote.

## VENUS SPACE PROBES

The National Aeronautics and Space Administration (NASA) launches two space probes: *Pioneer 1* in May, and *Pioneer 2* in August. They go into orbit around the planet Venus in December and map the surface using radar.

## CFCs BANNED

The use of chlorofluorocarbons (CFCs) is banned in the United States and Sweden because they are thought to be harming the ozone layer. CFCs are synthetic chemicals used as propellants in aerosols, refrigerants in refrigerators and air conditioners, and in the manufacture of foam boxes used for take-out foods.

## VIRUS GENES EXAMINED

The genome (genetic structure) of Virus SV40 is worked out, the first organism to be examined and mapped in this way.

## GOLDA MEIR
### (1898–1978)

Former Israeli prime minister Golda Meir has died. Born in Russia, she lived in the United States before settling in Palestine in 1921. Having been involved in the Labor Movement, she became Israeli ambassador to the Soviet Union on the founding of the new state. In 1949, she became a government minister and in 1969 was elected prime minister. She resigned after the fourth Arab-Israeli war in 1974.

## EVITA

A new musical, composed by Andrew Lloyd Webber with lyrics by Tim Rice, has opened. Called *Evita*, it is based on the life of Argentinian leader Eva Perón and achieves international success.

## SUPERMAN THE MOVIE

Starring Christopher Reeve and directed by Richard Donner, a new movie, *Superman*, has opened. Featuring wonderful special effects, it is one of the most expensive films ever made.

## VIETNAM INVADES CAMBODIA

Vietnam invades Cambodia to overthrow the Khmer Rouge government. The Vietnamese seize the capital, Phnom Penh, in January and install the rebel leader, Heng Samrin, in power. The discovery of the killing fields, where the Khmer Rouge disposed of their millions of victims, causes international outrage. Despite their fall from power, Khmer Rouge rebels keep up armed resistance until their leader Pol Pot dies, probably by suicide, in 1998.

## TRANSATLANTIC BALLOON FLIGHT

Three U.S. businessmen complete the first manned transatlantic balloon crossing from the United States to France in 137 hours and 18 minutes.

## INTERNATIONAL WOMEN'S DAY

March 8 is officially International Women's Day. Seventy years ago, on March 8, 1908, hundreds of women clothing workers in New York City demanded the vote. In 1910, the Socialist Women's International led by German feminist Clara Zetkin (1857–1933), named the date International Women's Day. Now the United Nations has made it official.

## TALES OF THE CITY

Armistead Maupin publishes *Tales of the City*. Stories of life in San Francisco, they began as a regular feature in the *San Francisco Chronicle*. Now they appear in book form for the first time, bringing Maupin widespread recognition.

## MASS SUICIDE

More than 900 members of the People's Temple, a religious cult under the leadership of the Reverend Jim Jones, located in the rain forest of Guyana, commit mass suicide. The dead include adults and children, who have died by drinking cyanide, some under duress.

## VERSATILE FOOD PROCESSOR

The Magimix electronic food processor comes on to the market. Designed in France, it combines several functions, such as blending, shredding, chopping, and even kneading, in one operation.

## DYSON CLEANER

Centrifugal force is harnessed by British inventor James Dyson to extract dust and dirt from the industrial or household environment. His Dual Cyclone is the first alternative to the vacuum cleaner since Hoover's first suction cleaner appeared in 1908.

## SKATEBOARDING CRAZE

Teenagers have taken up a new craze — skateboarding. Sidewalks and parks in both America and Britain are full of young people performing skateboarding stunts.

## ARGENTINA BEATS HOLLAND

The Dutch, for the second consecutive time, fall to the home country in the final game of the soccer World Cup. Argentina beats them 3–1.

## ALI VICTORIOUS

U.S. boxing star Muhammad Ali beats Leon Spinks, who had taken the title from him, to regain the heavyweight boxing crown for an unprecedented third time.

## IRONMAN RACE

The Ironman race in Hawaii begins when sports enthusiasts combine a 2.4 mile swim, an 112 mile bike race, and a 26 mile marathon to find the best all-round athlete. The race has grown from small beginnings to become a prestige event and has spawned other, shorter triathlons.

## JOMO KENYATTA
### (c.1889–1978)

Kenyan leader Jomo Kenyatta has died. The former herd boy, who eventually studied at London University, was president of the Pan-African Federation. From 1946, he was president of the Kenyan African Union. He was the Kikuyu people's Mau Mau leader during the struggles for repossession of their lands and was imprisoned from 1952–1959. He became prime minister in 1963 in the period up to independence and became president in 1964.

# REVOLUTION IN IRAN

The Shah of Iran flees into exile. Fundamentalist Iranian spiritual leader Ayatollah Khomeini takes over and U.S. hostages are seized. The Sandinistas gain victory in Nicaragua. The U.S.S.R. invades Afghanistan. Idi Amin's rule comes to an end in Uganda. A potentially catastrophic accident at Three Mile Island in Pennsylvania draws attention to the dangers of nuclear power. Space probes send back photographs of Venus and Saturn and a tiny personal stereo, the Sony Walkman, goes on sale.

## 1 9 7 9

| | | |
|---|---|---|
| **Jan** | 8 | Vietnamese occupy Phnom Penh, Cambodia, overthrowing Khmer Rouge regime |
| | 21 | Terry Bradshaw leads the Pittsburgh Steelers in defeating the Dallas Cowboys 35-31, the first rematch in Super Bowl history |
| | 30 | Shah of Iran flees into exile and the Ayatollah Khomeini will be returning to power |
| **Mar** | 26 | Israel and Egypt sign peace treaty |
| | 28 | Major accident occurs at Three Mile Island nuclear plant |
| **April** | 2 | Mass graves are discovered in northeast Cambodia, evidence of mass murders carried out by Khmer Rouge |
| | 11 | Tanzanian forces overthrow Ugandan dictator Idi Amin |

| | | |
|---|---|---|
| **May** | 3 | Margaret Thatcher is elected the first British woman Prime Minister |
| **June** | 18 | U.S.S.R. and U.S. sign Strategic Arms Limitation Treaty (SALT 2) |
| **July** | 25 | General Somoza flees Nicaragua after Sandinista victory |
| **Aug** | 30 | WW II hero Earl Mountbatten of Burma is killed by an IRA bomb |
| **Nov** | 4 | Followers of Ayatollah Khomeini seize U.S. embassy in Tehran and take hostages |
| **Dec** | 10 | Mother Teresa wins the Nobel Peace Prize |
| | 24 | First successful launch of European Space Agency's rocket, *Ariane* |
| | 27 | U.S.S.R. invades Afghanistan |

## ISLAMIC REVOLUTION IN IRAN

The Shah flees into exile in Egypt as supporters of the fundamentalist religious leader, Ayatollah Khomeini (1900–1989), seize power. His flight follows months of demonstrations and unrest and is greeted with enormous celebration. The ayatollah returns from exile in Paris and institutes an Islamic republic. In November, students seize the U.S. embassy in Tehran and take its 63 U.S. staff and 40 other people hostage, demanding the return of the Shah for trial. The crisis leads to a confrontation between Iran and the United States. The hostages are not released until January 1981, after 444 days in captivity.

## SANDINISTA VICTORY

Fighting breaks out again in Nicaragua. This time the Marxist Sandinistas are better armed and equipped by Cuba. By July, they have ousted Nicaraguan dictator General Anastastio Somoza, who flees to the U.S. This brings to an end a cruel and corrupt dictatorship. The Sandinista rebels, named after a revolutionary leader killed in the 1930s, form a provisional government.

## IRANIAN WOMEN PROTEST

March 8, International Women's Day, is marked by protests by Iranian women against strict Islamic laws introduced under Ayatollah Khomeini.

## THREE MILE ISLAND

A major accident occurs at Three Mile Island nuclear power station in Pennsylvania. Owing to a technical error, a nuclear reactor overheats, causing the release of some radioactive gas. The possibility of a total meltdown causes the evacuation of thousands of people. The crisis is averted, but it is the worst nuclear accident in the United States and alerts people to the possible dangers of nuclear power.

## THE CHINA SYNDROME

American actress Jane Fonda (b. 1937) stars as the journalist investigating the story of a meltdown at a nuclear reactor in the new film, *The China Syndrome*. The title comes from the fire which, it is said, could theoretically burn through the Earth to China. The film gains new topicality after the accident at the power plant at Three Mile Island.

## UGANDAN CIVIL WAR

Ugandan dictator Idi Amin (1925-2003) has annexed the Kagera area of northern Tanzania, near the Ugandan border. Tanzanian president Julius Nyerere (b. 1922) sends troops to support the Uganda National Liberation Army (UNLA) which has been formed to fight the dictatorial and increasingly bloodthirsty Idi Amin. As they approach Kampala, Libyan troops who have come to Amin's assistance, attack and halt them briefly, but UNLA takes the capital and Amin is forced to flee. A civilian government returns to power.

## CHINA INVADES VIETNAM

Chinese forces invade the Cao Bang area of northern Vietnam to punish the country for its invasion of Cambodia. The Chinese are fought to a standstill and forced to withdraw after suffering 20,000 killed or wounded. Vietnamese casualties are estimated to be 27,000 killed or wounded.

## APOCALYPSE NOW

Directed by Francis Ford Coppola (b. 1939), the film *Apocalypse Now* is a loose adaptation of Joseph Conrad's novel *Heart of Darkness*, set in the Vietnam War. The film stuns audiences with its images of helicopters and warfare and its gripping tale of Captain Benjamin Willard's (Martin Sheen) quest for Kurtz (Marlon Brando).

ABOVE AND LEFT: Gays and lesbians march on Washington to demand human rights.

ABOVE: The mellow proprietor of a real drugstore in Washington, D.C. The shops sells marijuana and the equipment needed to use it.

### THATCHER VICTORY
Margaret Thatcher (b. 1925) becomes the first British woman prime minister when her Conservative Party wins the general election. She embarks on a right-wing, free market policy of privatization of state assets and a tough anti-trade union policy.

### SALT-2
U.S. president Carter (b. 1924) and Soviet leader Leonid Brezhnev (1906–82) sign the SALT-2 (Strategic Arms Limitation Talks) Treaty, agreeing to restrict each side to 2,250 strategic nuclear missiles. The deal is never ratified by the U.S. Senate and is abandoned as the arms race intensifies during the early 1980s.

### POSTMODERNISM
Jean-François Lyotard publishes a new study summing up a distanced, ironic approach to art and literature, which comes to be known as postmodernism. The term will be widely used in the coming decade.

### SOVIET UNION INVADES AFGHANISTAN
Intending to make a quick change in government, Soviet president Leonid Breshnev sends 55,000 troops into Afghanistan to oust President Hafizullah Amin and replace him with a new Afghan leader, Babrak Karmal. This leads to a drawn-out guerrilla war. The Communist coup is opposed by fundamentalist Muslim tribal groups, who are assisted by the United States.

### PEDALING OVER THE CHANNEL
In June, the 77 pound airplane *Gossamer Albatross* flies across the English Channel. It is powered by U.S. biologist Bryan Allen, who drives the propeller using bicycle-type pedals.

### THE DINNER PARTY
American feminist and artist Judy Chicago's multimedia creation, *The Dinner Party*, goes on exhibit. A tribute to women's history, it takes the form of a triangular table with 39 symbolic place settings, each representing a key woman. The whole thing is positioned on a floor inscribed with the names of 999 other women of note.

### PHOTOGRAPHS FROM SPACE
Photographs of Saturn are transmitted by U.S. space probe *Pioneer 11*, launched in 1973. *Voyager 1*, launched in 1977 to take advantage of an alignment of Jupiter, Saturn, Uranus, and Neptune, transmitted photographs of Jupiter's rings in March. Passing within 3,000 miles of each planet's surface, *Voyager 1* and *2* discover Jupiter's powerful magnetic field and its continuous thunderstorms. They also photograph the planet's moons.

### AIR-CUSHIONED SNEAKERS
The first air-cushioned sneaker is developed by engineer Frank Rudy at Nike. The company was formed in 1967 to market track shoes with nylon uppers developed by William J. Bowerman, the track coach at the University of Oregon. These will become a style statement for young people.

LEFT: Israeli leader Menachem Begin signing the Middle East peace agreement at Camp David. President Jimmy Carter, architect of the agreement, looks on.

RIGHT: The accident at Three Mile Island nuclear reactor polarizes opinion on the usefulness and safety of nuclear power. Thousands take to the streets to protest.

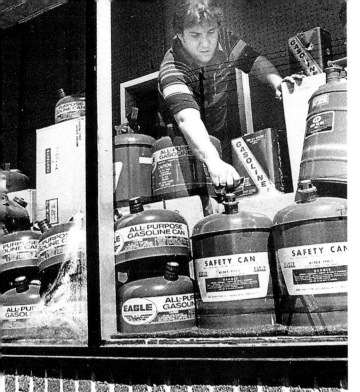

ABOVE: American automobiles line up for gas during the politically inspired oil crisis that slows down the late 1970s.

LEFT: Smart shop owners stockpile cans of gas in anticipation of panic buying by their customers.

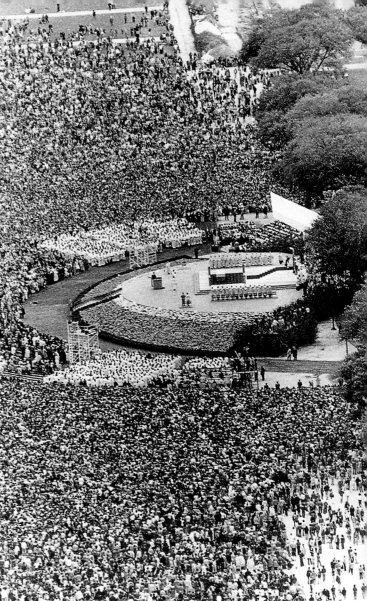

## SKYLAB CRASHES
The U.S. space station *Skylab I* falls back to Earth. It has traveled 87 million miles in orbit since its launch in 1973.

## GLUONS DETECTED
U.S. scientists detect the existence of subatomic particles that hold quarks together. They are called gluons.

## PEACE PRIZE
Mother Teresa (1910–1997), an Albanian Roman Catholic nun, founder of the Missionaries of Charity religious order who works among the poor in Calcutta, is awarded the Nobel Peace Prize.

## WALKMANS
The Japanese company, Sony, has launched the Sony Walkman, a portable personal stereo cassette player with headphones. It is so small that you can listen to music anywhere, even when walking around the streets.

OPPOSITE ABOVE: Disco fever still rages at the terminally hip New York City night clubs.

OPPOSITE BELOW: Two years after *Saturday Night Fever*, young hopefuls still dance for prizes.

ABOVE AND ABOVE LEFT: Pope John Paul II comes to the United States and celebrates mass on the Mall in Washington, D.C.

## NEW DINOSAUR CLUE
U.S. scientists Luis and Walter Alvarez discover traces of a huge meteorite impact some 65 million years ago. They propose that dust from it may have changed the climate and caused the extinction of the dinosaurs.

## EL SALVADOR REBELS
A communist guerrilla movement, the Farabundo Marti Liberation Front (FMLN), wages war against El Salvador's right-wing government.

## ROLLERBLADING
Brothers Scott and Brennan Olsen create the first popular Rollerblade or in-line skate in Minneapolis. Keen ice skaters, they wanted to be able to practice in summer.

## KKK KILLS FOUR
Two carloads of 12 Ku Klux Klan members opened fire on demonstrators in Greensboro, N.C. who were opposing the Klan, killing four people and wounding eight others.

# WINNERS AND ACHIEVERS OF THE 1970s

## ACADEMY AWARDS

The Academy of Motion Picture Arts and Sciences was founded in 1927 by the movie industry to honor its artists and craftsmen. All categories of motion picture endeavor are honored, but the most significant are listed below.

### BEST ACTOR
**1970** George C Scott *Patton*
**1971** Gene Hackman *The French Connection*
**1972** Marlon Brando *The Godfather*
**1973** Jack Lemmon *Save the Tiger*
**1974** Art Carney *Harry and Tonto*
**1975** Jack Nicholson *One Flew Over the Cuckoo's Nest*
**1976** Peter Finch *Network*
**1977** Richard Dreyfuss *The Goodbye Girl*
**1978** Jon Voight *Coming Home*
**1979** Dustin Hoffman *Kramer vs. Kramer*

### BEST ACTRESS
**1970** Glenda Jackson *Women in Love*
**1971** Jane Fonda *Klute*
**1972** Liza Minnelli *Cabaret*
**1973** Glenda Jackson *A Touch of Class*
**1974** Ellen Burstyn *Alice Doesn't Live Here Anymore*
**1975** Louise Fletcher *One Flew Over the Cuckoo's Nest*
**1976** Faye Dunaway *Network*
**1977** Diane Keaton *Annie Hall*
**1978** Jane Fonda *Coming Home*
**1979** Sally Field *Norma Rae*

### BEST DIRECTOR
**1970** Franklin J Schaffner *Patton*
**1971** William Friedkin *The French Connection*
**1972** Bob Fosse *Cabaret*
**1973** George Roy Hill *The Sting*
**1974** Francis Ford Coppola *The Godfather, Part II*
**1975** Milos Forman *One Flew Over the Cuckoo's Nest*
**1976** John Avildsen *Rocky*
**1977** Woody Allen *Annie Hall*
**1978** Michael Cimino *The Deer Hunter*
**1979** Robert Benton *Kramer vs. Kramer*

### BEST PICTURE
**1970** *Patton*
**1971** *The French Connection*
**1972** *The Godfather*
**1973** *The Sting*
**1974** *The Godfather, Part II*
**1975** *One Flew Over the Cuckoo's Nest*
**1976** *Rocky*
**1977** *Annie Hall*
**1978** *The Deer Hunter*
**1979** *Kramer vs. Kramer*

## NOBEL PRIZES

The Nobel Prizes are an international award granted in the fields of literature, physics, chemistry, physiology or medicine, and peace. The first prizes were awarded in 1901 and funded by the money left in the will of the Swedish inventor Alfred Nobel (1833–1896), who gave the world dynamite.

### PRIZES FOR LITERATURE
**1970** Alexander Solzhenitsyn (Soviet) for fiction
**1971** Pablo Neruda (Chilean) for poetry
**1972** Heinrich Böll (German) for fiction and drama
**1973** Patrick White (Australian) for fiction
**1974** Eyvind Johnson (Swedish) for fiction and Harry Edmund Martinson (Swedish) for essays, drama, fiction and poetry
**1975** Eugenio Montale (Italian) for poetry
**1976** Saul Bellow (American) for fiction
**1977** Vicente Aleixandre (Spanish) for poetry
**1978** Isaac Bashevis Singer (Polish-born) for fiction
**1979** Odysseus Elytis (Greek) for poetry

### PRIZES FOR PEACE
**1970** Norman Borlaug (American) for developing high-yield grains to increase food in developing countries
**1971** Willy Brandt (German) for efforts to improve relations between Communist and non-Communist nations
**1972** *No award*
**1973** Henry Kissinger (American) and Le Duc Tho (North Vietnamese) for work in negotiating the Vietnam War cease-fire agreement (Le Duc Tho declined)
**1974** Sean MacBride (Irish) for working to guarantee human rights through international law, and Eisaku Sato (Japanese) for efforts to improve international relations and stop the spread of nuclear weapons
**1975** Andrei Sakharov (Soviet) for work in promoting peace and opposing violence and brutality.
**1976** Mairead Corrigan and Betty Williams (Irish) for organizing a movement to end Protestant-Catholic fighting in Northern Ireland (award delayed until 1977
**1977** Amnesty International for helping political prisoners

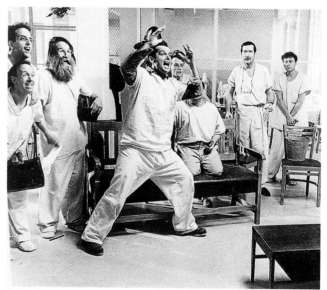

Jack Nicholson is shown in *One Flew Over the Cuckoo's Nest*, which swept the board in 1975, winning Best Film, Best Director, and Best Actor.

**1978** Menachem Begin (Israeli) and Anwar el-Sadat (Egyptian) for efforts to end the Arab-Israeli conflict.
**1979** Mother Teresa (Rumanian born) for aiding India's poor.

### PRIZES FOR PHYSICS
**1970** Hannes Olof Goast Alfven (Swedish) for work in magneto-hydrodynamics, the study of electrical and magnetic effects in fluids that conduct electricity, and Louis Eugêne Felix Neel (French) for discoveries of magnetic properties that applied to computer memories
**1971** Dennis Gabor (British) for work in holography
**1972** John Bardeen, Leon Cooper, and John Robert Schrieffer (American) for work on superconductivity, the disappearance of electrical resistance
**1973** Ivar Giaever (American), Leo Esaki (Japanese) and Brian Josephson (British) for work on electron "tunneling" through semiconductor and superconductor materials
**1974** Antony Hewish (British) for the discovery of pulsars, and Sir Martin Ryle (British) for the use of small radio telescopes to "see" into space with great accuracy
**1975** L. James Rainwater (American) and Aage Bohr and Ben Mottelson (Danish) for work on the structure of the atomic nucleus
**1976** Burton Richter and Samuel Chao Chung Ting (American) for discovery of an elementary nuclear particle called the psi, or J particle

**1977** Philip W. Anderson and John Van Vleck (American) and Sir Nevill Mott (British) for helping develop semiconductor devices
**1978** Pyotr Kapitsa (Soviet) for research in low-temperature physics, and Arno Penzias and Robert Wilson (American) for the discovery and study of cosmic microwave background radiation
**1979** Sheldon Glashow and Steven Weinberg (American) and Abdus Salam (Pakistani) for developing a principle that unifies the weak nuclear force and the force of electromagnetism

### PRIZES FOR CHEMISTRY
**1970** Luis Federico Leloir (Argentine) for the discovery of chemical compounds that affect the storage of chemical energy in living things
**1971** Gerhard Herzberg (Canadian) for research on the structure of molecules, particularly on free radicals
**1972** Christian B. Anfinsen, Stanford Moore and William H Stein (American) for fundamental contributions to the chemistry of enzymes
**1973** Geoffrey Wilkinson (British) and Ernst Fischer (German) for work on organometallic compounds
**1974** Paul John Flory (American) for work in polymer chemistry
**1975** John Warcup Cornforth (Australian-born) and Vladimir Prelog (Swiss) for work on the chemical synthesis of organic compounds

# WINNERS AND ACHIEVERS OF THE 1970s

**1976** William Lipscomb, Jr. (American) for studies on the structure and bonding mechanisms of boranes, complex compounds of boron and hydrogen
**1977** Ilya Prigogine (Belgian) for contributions to non equilibrium thermodynamics
**1978** Peter Mitchell (British) for studies of cellular energy transfer
**1979** Herbert Brown (American) and George Wittig (German) for developing compounds capable of producing chemical bonds

## PRIZES FOR PHYSIOLOGY OR MEDICINE

**1970** Julius Axelrod (American), Bernard Katz (British) and Ulf Svante von Euler (Swedish) for discoveries of the role played by certain chemicals in the transmission of nerve impulses
**1971** Earl W. Sutherland Jr. (American) for the discovery of the ways hormones act, including the discovery of cyclic AMP, a chemical that influences the actions of hormones on body processes
**1972** Gerald M. Edelman (American) and Rodney Porter (British) for discovering the chemical structure of antibodies
**1973** Nikolaas Tinbergen (Dutch-born) and Konrad Lorenz and Karl von Frisch (Austrian) for their studies on animal behavior
**1974** Christian de Duve (Belgian) and Albert Claude and George E.. Palade (American) for pioneer work in cell biology
**1975** David Baltimore, Renato Dulbecco and Howard M Temin (American) for research on how certain viruses affect the genes of cancer cells
**1976** Baruch S. Blumberg and D. Carleton Gajdusek (American) for discoveries concerning the origin and spread of infectious diseases
**1977** Roger Guillemin, Andrew Schally and Rosalyn Yalow (American) for research into hormones
**1978** Werner Arber (Swiss) and Daniel Nathans and Hamilton O. Smith

(American) for discoveries in molecular genetics
**1979** Allan Macleod Cormack (American) and Godfrey Newbold Hounsfield (British) for contributions to the development of the computerized tomographic (CT) scanner

## WORLD CUP FINAL MATCHES

| YEAR | LOCATION |
|------|----------|
| **1970** | **Mexico City** |

Brazil defeats Italy 4-1
| **1974** | **Munich** |

West Germany defeats Netherlands 2-1
| **1978** | **Buenos Aires** |

Argentina defeats Netherlands 3-1

## SITES OF THE OLYMPIC GAMES

**1972** SUMMER Munich, Germany
WINTER Sapporo, Japan
**1976** SUMMER Montreal, Canada
WINTER Innsbruck, Austria

## U.S. PRESIDENTS

**1969–1974** President Richard Milhous Nixon, *Republican*
1969–1973 Vice President Spiro T. Agnew; 1973–1974 Vice President Gerald R Ford
**1974–1977** President Gerald Rudolph Ford, *Republican*
1974–1977 Vice President Nelson A. Rockefeller
**1977–1981** President James Earl Carter, *Democrat*
1977–1981 Vice President Walter F. Mondale

## INDIANAPOLIS 500

**1970** Al Unser, Sr.
**1971** Al Unser, Sr.
**1972** Mark Donohue
**1973** Gordon Johncock
**1974** Johnny Rutherford
**1975** Bobby Unser
**1976** Johnny Rutherford
**1977** A.J. Foyt, Jr.
**1978** Al Unser, Sr.
**1979** Rick Mears

## KENTUCKY DERBY WINNERS

**1970** Dust Commander
**1971** Canonero II
**1972** Riva Ridge
**1973** Secretariat
**1974** Cannonade
**1975** Foolish Pleasure
**1976** Bold Forbes
**1977** Seattle Slew
**1978** Affirmed
**1979** Spectacular Bid

## NBA CHAMPIONS

**1970** New York Knicks defeat Los Angeles Lakers
**1971** Milwaukee Bucks defeat Baltimore Bullets
**1972** Los Angeles Lakers defeat New York Knicks
**1973** New York Knicks defeat Los Angeles Lakers
**1974** Boston Celtics defeat Milwaukee Bucks
**1975** Golden State Warriors defeat Washington Bullets
**1976** Boston Celtics defeat Phoenix Suns
**1977** Portland Trail Blazers defeat Philadelphia 76ers
**1978** Washington Bullets defeat Seattle SuperSonics
**1979** Seattle SuperSonics defeat Washington Bullets

## SUPER BOWL CHAMPIONS

**1970** Kansas City Chiefs defeat Minnesota Vikings
**1971** Baltimore Colts defeat Dallas Cowboys
**1972** Dallas Cowboys defeat Miami Dolphins
**1973** Miami Dolphins defeat Washington Redskins
**1974** Miami Dolphins defeat Minnesota Vikings
**1975** Pittsburgh Steelers defeat Minnesota Vikings
**1976** Pittsburgh Steelers defeat Dallas Cowboys

**1977** Oakland Raiders defeat Minnesota Vikings
**1978** Dallas Cowboys defeat Denver Broncos
**1979** Pittsburgh Steelers defeat Dallas Cowboys

## WIMBLEDON CHAMPIONS

**1970** MEN John Newcombe
WOMEN Margaret Smith Court
**1971** MEN John Newcombe
WOMEN Evonne Goolagong
**1972** MEN Stan Smith
WOMEN Billie Jean King
**1973** MEN Jan Kodes
WOMEN Billie Jean King
**1974** MEN Jimmy Connors
WOMEN Chris Evert
**1975** MEN Arthur Ashe
WOMEN Billie Jean King
**1976** MEN Bjorn Borg
WOMEN Chris Evert
**1977** MEN Bjorn Borg
WOMEN Virginia Wade
**1978** MEN Bjorn Borg
WOMEN Martina Navratilova
**1979** MEN BJORN BORG
WOMEN Martina Navratilova

## WORLD SERIES CHAMPIONS

**1970** Baltimore Orioles defeat Cincinnati Reds
**1971** Pittsburgh Pirates defeat Baltimore Orioles
**1972** Oakland Athletics defeat Cincinnati Reds
**1973** Oakland Athletics defeat New York Mets
**1974** Oakland Athletics defeat Los Angeles Dodgers
**1975** Cincinnati Reds defeat Boston Red Sox
**1976** Cincinnati Reds defeat New York Yankees
**1977** New York Yankees defeat Los Angeles Dodgers
**1978** New York Yankees defeat Los Angeles Dodgers
**1979** Pittsburgh Pirates defeat Baltimore Orioles